HOW TO FIND, RECRUIT & MANAGE INDEPENDENT SALES AGENTS

A GUIDE BOOK FOR COMPANIES LOOKING TO EXPAND INTO NEW MARKETS WITHOUT THE HIGH COST OF HIRING A DIRECT SALES FORCE!

ROBERT J. WEESE

MANAGING PARTNER
B2B SALES CONNECTIONS

ISBN: 978-0-9876928-3-2

DEDICATION

To Mom - You encouraged us to learn, play music, take chances, help others, explore and always be home before the streetlights came on.

Learn Techniques Used By Top Performing Companies To Create Your Own Successful Sales Agent Program

Are you struggling to grow your sales?

Are you trying to decide whether the time is right to hire a direct sales force?

Would you like to approach new markets and territories using a proven business model that will reduce your go-to-market costs?

HOW TO FIND, RECRUIT & MANAGE INDEPENDENT SALES AGENTS
will help you achieve your goals by giving you a step by step process for developing a successful sales agent program.

Testimonials:

"This fast-moving, practical book, based on years of experience, shows you how to leverage and multiply the sales potential of your products and services, selling five and ten times as much as you ever thought possible."
Brian Tracy – Author, Ultimate Sales Success

"Bob has written a comprehensive guide which offers the reader a complete review of how to select, manage and motivate independent reps. He provides proven exercises, forms, and templates to equip interested sales managers with the necessary tools to run their own successful sales agent program. This book is essential reading for anyone interested in the independent sales rep business model."
Allan R. Lambert, CSP Billiken Group, LLC

"Manufacturers need to learn more about how the rep business functions before they approach someone. They need to talk to other companies that use rep's or attend one of the MRERF programs. Unfortunately, only a very small percentage of companies know about reps."
Karen Jefferson, CPMR CSP Executive Director, MRERF

"As more companies are looking for cost savings you are going to see a move towards more sales outsourcing. The agent business is poised for growth. Agents are going to play a very important role as more international companies are trying to break into the North American market."
Pierre Carriere, President BEXSA Solutions Inc.

"More and more large companies are finding their direct sales force is a huge expense. Cost of sales is rising and the ramp up time for a new sales person can take months or more. With agents getting paid on results it really makes sense for companies to consider this sales channel."
Craig Lindsay, CPMR CSP President Pacesetter Sales & Associates

"In my experience, the formula is relatively simple. Reps want to work with companies that provide collaborative support and partnership that will complement their efforts. The companies that do this the best will get and hold onto the best reps and rep groups."
David Lane, General Manager at A1A Management LLC

Part of the Series
Action Plan for Sales Success

Contents

"Success is not a matter of looking for opportunities,
It's based on creating the opportunity"

Chapter 1 - A New Look At Hiring Sales People

Fred Ford is the owner of Riff Raff Manufacturing Inc. In 10 years he has built his company from a simple idea based on a market need, into a $2 million dollar a year business. Fred is a technical guy, he understands how to build his product and he understands what his customers need but sales and marketing skills are not his forte. For the first 8 years Fred was responsible for all of the company's sales and he succeeded in spite of his poor selling skills. Customers bought his products and Fred enjoyed a good lifestyle. Word of mouth and referrals were the company's bread and butter. Customers who knew Fred or needed his unique product contacted him directly to order the products. As Fred put it "I'm more an order taker than a salesman." Selling was easy. The customers had a need and Fred had the right product for them.

Then things changed. Sales reached a plateau and new competitors entered the market and started to approach his long term customers and cut into his business. Fred knew something had to be done and he decided to hire a full time sales person. The goal was to find someone to work with his existing customers to improve communications, build sales and look for new customers who could benefit from Riff Raff's products.

That's when the problems started. Fred had never hired a sales person and was not sure how to do it or even what to expect. He didn't know what he was doing. Then he had a break. Dave, a family friend who had recently left his job, approached Fred and suggested he had the experience and the connections to be Fred's sales person. This appeared to be a real coup. Fred was getting an experienced sales person whom he knew and trusted without the headaches associated with trying to hire someone unknown. Fred saw this as a win-win. He hired an experienced sales person and helped out his friend at the same time.

Unfortunately, this is where the good news ends and the problems began. Dave joined the company and parked himself at his new desk in his new office. Fred suggested he should start by visiting their current customers and then contact potential customers in the same markets. Dave thought that was a great idea and for the first few weeks he met with customers and prospects in an attempt to generate sales but he had very little success renewing current customers or signing up new accounts.

Then the excuses started. Dave complained the marketing material was not good so he decided to spend the next few weeks updating the company brochures. That led to website changes that he took care of personally. This added more weeks to the marketing project. Dave then reported that new prospects were complaining about the price of the products and service issues were preventing sales. Just about every excuse you could imagine was given for declining sales. The result was Dave spent fewer and fewer hours selling and more and more time focused on make-work marketing projects in order to avoid customer contact.

Fred became frustrated with the situation. He was paying Dave a substantial salary and he could not afford to continue to support him without an improvement in sales. Fred spoke to his wife and a few close friends about the problem and they all felt that Dave was a great guy who obviously knew what he was doing. Surely it would result in even better sales in the near future once the marketing project was completed. Fred hoped this was the case but secretly believed that he had made a mistake giving Dave the job.

The months passed by quickly and sales did not improve. Dave grew more and more defensive every time Fred asked what he was doing or wanted to discuss sales forecasts and opportunities in the pipeline. Dave always had a long list of 'potential' accounts but none were closing and he became even more defensive. Dave had all the excuses. Prices were too high, the competition was killing them, customers couldn't make decisions and Riff Raff had serious problems with customer service according to Dave's view of the situation.

Fred knew it was time to make a change but firing Dave would mean admitting he had made a mistake in the first place and it would also cause conflict in his family since Dave was a longtime friend.

Finally, almost 14 months after he first hired Dave, Fred decided it was time to broach the subject and ask Dave to leave. As you can imagine, it didn't go well. Dave was furious and threatened to sue Fred. The gloves came off and weeks later, after spending thousands of dollars in legal fees, Dave was gone.

The story of Fred and Dave is nothing new to small business owners. Most companies have made hiring mistakes when they recruited new sales people. Whether it's from lack of experience or trusting others too much, it happens frequently. In my sales career I have heard this story repeated hundreds of times. Sometimes it's a friend, more often it's a family member who comes to the rescue only to make things worse in the long run both for the business and the family.

Fred did not solve his problem, which was the need for more sales. Instead he caused a whole new series of problems that required his focus before he could get back to the challenge of how to rebuild his sales.

It was then that I met Fred and learned of his situation. He had a great product which was still in demand but his local market was shrinking and he needed to expand his selling efforts beyond his current marketplace. He had customers in other parts of the country and when speaking with them he found out there were many more potential buyers for his products. All he had to do was find a better way to connect with them.

That's when we started talking about independent sales agents (ISA's or sales agents). They are found all across the nation and in many other countries around the world. The beauty of sales agents is they work on straight commission and already have contacts in the companies that Fred was looking to approach. By teaming up with a few sales agents in key territories Fred could quickly expand his market penetration and have the agents connect their customers with his company. Best of all, the sales agents would only be paid on sales once they were completed. No salary, no benefits, no expenses.

It has been said; 'sales agents are the hired guns of the sales industry.' If they believe your product or service will help them grow their business and will be a benefit to their customers, then they will want to be your representative in their territory.

After his initial research and discussions with companies that had used sales agents, Fred was convinced. The cost of finding and recruiting independent sales agents was relatively inexpensive compared to the potential return on his investment. With some direction and assistance we created a recruiting program and a training program for his new agents. A few months later Fred had a network of sales agents in place covering more territory that he ever thought would be possible.

After a short initial learning curve, each agent started to bring in a few thousand dollars in monthly sales. As Fred saw his sales improve he invested more time working with the agents and that focus, in turn, resulted in better sales growth. A few thousand dollars a month soon gave way to tens of thousands of dollars in new sales and once the agents started receiving regular commissions from the product line they redoubled their efforts and sales continued to grow. Within the first year the sales agents channel had his sales back to their previous levels and the second year he had doubled his business.

While Fred Ford and Riff Raff Manufacturing are fictional, this story is not. There are thousands of businesses in North America that have developed channels of independent sales agents either to replace their direct sales staff, or augment the direct sales channel in areas where a company could not afford to position their own people. Simply put, in many industries sales agents make good business sense.

By joining forces with sales agents who are currently selling to customers in your target market, you can ramp up your sales efforts faster and less expensively than if you try to hire and train a direct sales force to reach those same customers. Independent sales agents are inexpensive to use, and can quickly get your products in front of customers in markets that you don't currently service. It doesn't matter whether you are trying to expand across the country or internationally, there are sales agents in most industries and geographies who are on the lookout for new products or services that can enhance their current business model.

Regardless of whether your business has always relied on a direct sales force or you are just starting out and have no sales; you should understand that one of the most successful alternate sales channels available involves a partnership between your company and the use of independent sales agents. Unfortunately, there are not many people who know anything about independent sales agents and even if they know a little about the business model they have not seriously considered it as part of their sales strategy.

Many sales agents are successful, experienced, reliable, trusted experts in their field and they can provide a unique opportunity for you to reach a new market or penetrate a new territory at a fraction of the cost of hiring, training, managing, and paying your own dedicated sales force. Yes, reduced costs are a huge benefit of working with sales agents but their benefits extend far beyond the savings.

Sources estimates there are tens of thousands of independent sales agents in North America and some estimates put that number well over 100,000 strong and growing. In many manufacturing and IT sectors, sales agents are the backbone of their sales strategy. Some agents are solo entrepreneurs who operate their own business and others are part of large multi-rep agencies that are responsible for tens of millions of dollars in annual sales for the companies they represent. Regardless of their size and make up, they all share something in common. They are in the territories you would like to cover and they call on customers you want to reach.

Business owners are often very skilled at the production and operation components of their businesses but unfortunately, they usually lack the experience and skills required to market and sell their products. As a result they rely heavily on outdated sales processes and bad advice. Many business owners don't realize that there are innovative new opportunities for accelerating their companies' sales growth. They just have to know where to look for the right information and then be ready to make the changes required to implement the new strategy.

The problem most companies experience when they try to establish their own channel of independent sales agents is their lack of preparation and a poor understanding of the sales agent business model. Most business owners think all they have to do is contact a bunch of existing sales agents, tell them how great their product is and they will line up to sell it. This won't work.

You may be asking yourself, 'how do I find independent sales agents' and once I have found them what are the steps I need to take to make my program successful. Well that's where this book comes in. I have spent most of my career working with companies that sold their products or services through channels of dealers, resellers, VARS and independent sales agents. Understanding how to leverage alternate sales channels is the key to your company's success. Remember the old saying; "proper planning and preparation prevents poor performance". Nowhere is this more crucial than in the planning and preparation needed to establish a channel of independent sales agents.

In 2008 when my business partner and I founded B2B Sales Connections Inc. we had spent our careers working for companies that sold their products and services using independent dealers and independent sales agents. Initially our new company worked with a few manufacturers based in Canada, the United States and Europe who were looking to expand their sales into the North American marketplace.

At first these companies hired us to find and pre-screen sales agents and direct sales professionals for them. I often describe what we do as more of a dating service than a recruiting and training company. As more and more companies approached us to help them find sales agents we realized that most small and midsized businesses (SMBs') did not have a clear picture of what they needed to do to find, recruit, train and manage sales people or sales agents.

Most often their process was based on placing an ad in a trade publication or searching an on line sales agent job board, conducting one or two interviews and then deciding to work with an agent when their "gut feeling" told them who was the best person for the job. Once the sales agent became a business partner they were given a few glossy brochures, a price book, and business cards and expected to "get out and sell."

In the first few months there was very little communication between the two parties. Unfortunately both thought the other did not need any direction or feedback because they both knew what was expected of them. Over time the sales agent would become frustrated with the lack of direction, support and training and the business owner would become frustrated that the sales agent was not performing as expected. Months or years later the situation would not have improved and the relationship would usually end badly.

Something had to give. As more and more business owners and sales agents complained about the same recurring challenges, we realized that a change in thinking was needed. We first began by working with our clients to ensure they had a comprehensive job description that included a full disclosure of the objectives and accountabilities for the sales agent. We also created a sales playbook that would encompass all the steps the agent and company needed to cover in their sales process. Our goal was to put a step-by-step sales program in place for the company and the new sales agent. This way nothing was left to chance and both parties understood and agreed upon their role in building a successful business relationship.

As we worked with more and more companies that were establishing a sales agent channel, we kept repeating the same information over and over again. This in turn led to me write a white paper that outlined tips and techniques which companies could use to design their own sales process: *Framework for Finding Sales Agents* can be downloaded from our Download Centre at http://www.B2BSalesConnections.com. We gave this outline to any company that needed a reference tool to help them understand what was required and the process they needed to follow. As our information expanded the white paper soon morphed into the outline for this book.

There are a multitude of books, "how to manuals" and training programs that cover almost every aspect of the selling process. However, if you undertake a Google™ search you will quickly discover there is almost no documentation available for someone intent on building an alternate sales channel using independent sales agents or independent manufacturers' representatives.

The focus of this book, ***How to Find, Recruit & Manager Independent Sales Agents,*** is twofold. First, if you are trying to determine whether to expand into a new sales channel, we want to provide you with a thorough understanding of the options and implications of this decision. Our goal is to help you create a comprehensive program based on the knowledge and best practices of sales professionals who have spent most of their careers building and managing successful sales agent programs.

Our second goal is to provide you with the tools you will need to design and implement a fully functional alternate channel sales process utilizing independent sales agents, manufacturers' representatives or commission only sales agents.

Each chapter is filled with information, sample files and templates to help you design your own sales agent program. We have included check lists for the most important activities and specific tools to help you manage this process. Please be advised that the samples and templates are not meant to be used as legal documents and it is your responsibility to seek independent legal advice when drafting your own sales contracts, agreements, offer letters and any other documentation.

This book can be used on its own for designing your sales agent program or in conjunction with our *Action Based Sales Training* programs to create a comprehensive framework for your alternate sales channel process as well as the sales training programs you will need for your business partners. More information is available at http://www.b2bsalesconnections.com/sales_training.php

Know before you Act!

The secret to working with independent sales agents is to have a comprehensive alternate sales channel business model in place before you make your first contact with them. Sales agents are not interested in people approaching them with "half-baked" ideas and promises. You must learn the proper formula for finding, recruiting, managing and operating within the unique parameter of the agent's business model.

A word of caution before you launch into a new direction; you need to ask yourself if you are ready to commit the time, energy and resources required to make your sales agent program successful. If you are not willing to make this type of commitment then you can be sure your channel will either fail to launch or never be successful.

As a final word of advice, I would like to make the point that sales agent programs are only successful when you are willing to work towards a win- win- win outcome. This means you must create a win for the sales agent, a win for their customers, resulting in a win for your business. If you do it right, a sales agent program can place your product or service in front of hundreds if not thousands of customers and companies faster than you would ever have had the opportunity to connect with using a direct sales force.

If you are committed to selling your products or services through a channel of independent sales agents then you need to commit to the program and take action to implement the necessary steps. If you can't drive this program forward yourself then either look for a person who has experience working with alternate sales channels or find a service provider that can help you.

To build an agent channel you need trust, accountability from senior management, strong communications, a good product, the ability to support the program and a repeatable, documented system that you will follow. If you are missing any of these parts the channel will most likely either fail to launch or fail to last.

How you approach building your sales agent channel will determine your outcome. If you are committed to a successful program then you need to dedicate time, money and resources to the program.

I hope this book will help you create and launch a successful channel of independent sales agents for your business and I welcome your feedback.

Quick References

Throughout this training manual you will find a number of icons that are used to highlight specific information.

Sales Tool Box: This will identify a specific worksheet or document you can modify and use in the design of your sales agent channel program.

Sales Idea: This will highlight an important point of information or idea you may not have considered.

Warning: This symbol will point out some of the common problems and pitfalls you should watch out for in your channel program.

Action Items: This will recommend action items you should undertake to design and implement your own sales channel program.

Red Flag: Specifying areas which should be avoided or handled carefully with further advice from qualified individuals such as accountants or lawyers.

Visit us on line to download our support material

All of the sales tools and spreadsheets used in this book can be purchased separately in electronic format from our website http://www.B2BSalesConnections.com. This will allow you to quickly revise the spreadsheets for your own usage instead of having to recreate them manually. A copy of our sample sales agent agreement and recruiting checklist is also available. This sample agreement provides a framework you can modify and give to your lawyer so they can create your own legal document.

Chapter 2 –Sales Agents and Alternate Sales Channels

In this chapter we are going to focus on various sales channels and then review how most companies currently sell their products or services. If you are using a very simple sales and marketing strategy today, you most likely manufacturer your product and then rely on a direct sales force to get it to market. While this "go to market strategy" has been around since people first started selling, it is important to understand that there are many different models available. In the next few pages we will review a number of methods companies use to get their products or services to the customer. Which method is best? That will depend on your needs and the buying habits of your customers.

The Power of Independent Sales Agents

Every week I receive emails and phone calls from companies that are looking to hire independent sales agents. They almost always see this as a cheap way to expand their market penetration. They don't have a plan, they don't have a budget and they don't know what they need. It's the old problem – they don't know what they don't know. However, they are sure if they can just find a few good sales agents the whole operation will magically fall into place and they will start making money.

It doesn't work that way. It will always be true that "proper planning and preparation prevents poor performance." This is also true when creating an independent sales agent channel. The better the planning and execution on your part the better the results.

I have spent over 25 years working directly with independent sales agents and dealers in a multitude of sales roles. As the National Sales Manager for a multi-national company I managed a sales channel that produced incredible sales growth because we had a well-designed program that both the company and the agents followed. As the channel developed we enhanced the successful processes and eliminated the pieces that were either not working or ineffective. During the 7 years that I ran the program we averaged an annual growth rate of 39%. This was one of the highest growth divisions in the company and it was accomplished using a channel of independent sales agents.

Our success was not because we had a revolutionary product. In fact we sold business products that were becoming less and less popular because of new technologies and cheaper competitive products. However, in spite of the contraction of the market we continued to grow the business using sales agents. We knew how to attract, recruit, train and manage agents and most importantly we knew how to make them successful. As agents bought into our program and methods the channel grew and prospered. It was a win for the agents and a win for the company.

Sales agents can work for your business too but to be successful you need a compelling business model, a great success story, and yes, good agents on board.

On the other hand if you are looking at sales agents as an inexpensive alternative to hiring your own sales people, you may be disappointed in the results unless you commit to the program and follow the steps we have outlined in this book.

What is a Sales Channel?

In the simplest definition a sales channel is how a company sells its products or services to the end user. This could include a direct sales force, a telemarketing team, a network of retail stores, an online e-store or even catalogues sent out via direct mail. Most people are very familiar with both direct and indirect sales channels although they may not use the same terminology to describe its features.   For the sake of simplicity we will use the following two definitions for direct sales channel and indirect sales channel.

Direct Sales Channel:

A direct sales channel is where the manufacturer/principal or reseller/distributor sells the products or services directly to the end user via their own sales force. This is most often a team of sales professionals employed directly by the company. This could be an *"outside"* sales force that travels throughout a specific territory and calls directly on customers and prospects in primarily a one-on-one interaction.

The direct channel can also be made up of an *"inside"* sales force. This is characterized by telephone sales people who call existing customers and new prospects. In other companies, a direct sales force may refer to a sales clerk who services customers that visit a company's store to purchase products. Regardless of the job title, a direct sales representative is typically paid a salary or an hourly wage with the possibility to earn additional commissions and/or bonuses.

Another popular direct sales channel that has grown exponentially in the last few years is the corporate online e-store. An online channel allows a company to post their products or services on the internet and sell directly to the end user. This process is very effective in many markets and has been growing in popularity. The cost of sale is substantially lower than using a direct sales force; however it is not as effective for higher priced products or those with complex selling processes requiring more interaction with the customer.

Indirect Sales Channel:

An indirect or alternate sales channel is characterized by the company establishing a sales process by using independent companies or sales agents who are not directly employed by the company.

What's the difference between an independent sales agent and an independent dealer or reseller when selling my goods? Independent sales agents sell products on behalf of a manufacturer or principal and receive a commission on each sale. Typically a sales agent does not carry any inventory and the paperwork for a sales agreement is written on the manufacturer's contracts, not the agent's. The agent never takes title or ownership of the product nor do they have to be concerned with accounts receivable or accounts payable. The role of the sales agent is to focus on selling on behalf of the manufacturer or a group of non-competitive manufacturers.

On the other hand, an independent dealer buys a manufacturer's or principal's product, usually carries inventory and is responsible for all aspects of the business cycle. The dealers or resellers will purchase the products at a wholesale cost and then mark up the price for resale. The monetary difference between the cost price and the retail price is the dealer margin which the reseller retains as their portion of the profit.

Later in the chapter we will go into more detail and discuss a number of different types of indirect alternate sales channels. The key point to remember is that the independent sales agent is not an employee of the company and never takes title to the products they sell. They must sell in order to survive.

> Under employment law it is very important to have a clearly written agreement which lays out the relationship between the "principal" and the sales agent. If an individual is deemed in the eyes of the law to be an employee of your company you may end up with penalties for not collecting taxes, employment insurance premiums and other fees which are required in your local jurisdiction. If you are not sure of the specifics, contact a lawyer who specializes in employment law before you create your sales agent agreement.

> "You are hiring someone who already has the connections and the network. Clients want to talk to him. They know the agent and they look forward to his visits. If a company goes out and hires a regional sales manager directly, do you really think they will find one guy who has all the connections and experience that they can find in a rep firm that has been around for over 15 years."
>
> *Allan R. Lambert, CSP Billiken Group, LLC*

Channels Then and Now

With the dawn of the manufacturing era most companies saw the sales channel as a very simple process. The manufacturer or principal produced the goods and the sales teams went out and sold them directly to retail businesses which in turn would resell them to the customers. In some instances a manufacturer would sell directly to the ultimate customers. This was a very simple linear process with no "middle men" involved.

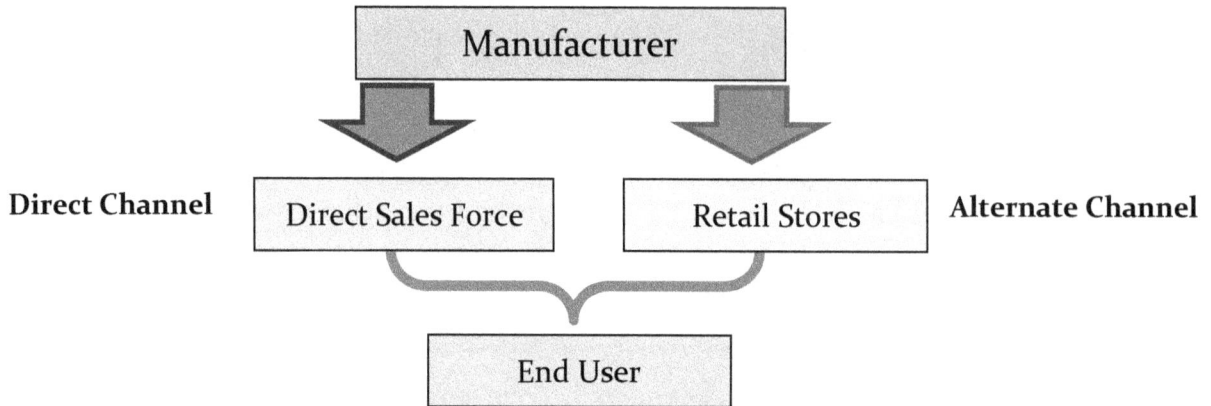

```
                        ┌─────────────────────┐
                        │    Manufacturer     │
                        └─────────────────────┘
                            ▼           ▼
Direct Channel    ┌──────────────────┐   ┌──────────────────┐    Alternate Channel
                  │ Direct Sales Force│   │   Retail Stores  │
                  └──────────────────┘   └──────────────────┘
                              ┌──────────────────┐
                              │     End User     │
                              └──────────────────┘
```

Today, the management of goods in even the smallest of organizations may be a very complex process. It can encompass direct sales channels which employ sales teams, catalogue sales, telephone sales teams, online e-stores or retail. Companies will often have a separate indirect sales channel comprised of private label or OEM brands for other companies, wholesalers, resellers, independent sales agents and retail stores.

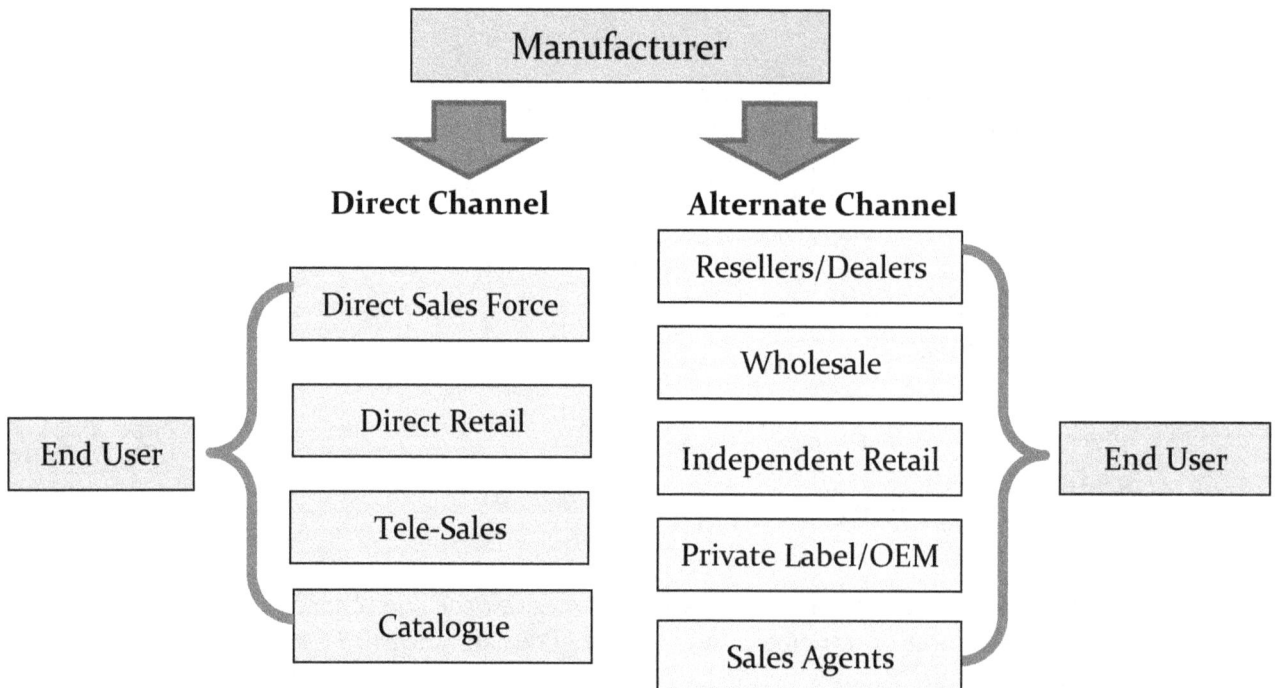

```
                        ┌─────────────────────┐
                        │    Manufacturer     │
                        └─────────────────────┘
                            ▼           ▼
                   Direct Channel      Alternate Channel
                                       ┌──────────────────┐
                                       │ Resellers/Dealers│
                   ┌──────────────────┐└──────────────────┘
                   │ Direct Sales Force│┌──────────────────┐
                   └──────────────────┘│    Wholesale     │
┌──────────┐       ┌──────────────────┐└──────────────────┘   ┌──────────┐
│ End User │       │   Direct Retail  │┌──────────────────┐   │ End User │
└──────────┘       └──────────────────┘│ Independent Retail│  └──────────┘
                   ┌──────────────────┐└──────────────────┘
                   │    Tele-Sales    │┌──────────────────┐
                   └──────────────────┘│ Private Label/OEM│
                   ┌──────────────────┐└──────────────────┘
                   │    Catalogue     │┌──────────────────┐
                   └──────────────────┘│   Sales Agents   │
                                       └──────────────────┘
```

As you can imagine, the opportunity to reach more customers is greatly enhanced by engaging in a more complex sales and distribution strategy, but it also compounds the problems when duplication occurs, especially if the channels begin to compete with one another and costs escalate.

Managing a direct sales channel allows you to set prices and control most aspects of the selling process. However, when you are working through a channel of independent sales agents you have to balance your need for control with the legal implications of using independent business people to represent your products.

What's the Best Channel for Your Product or Service?

Before you invest the time, energy and money required to create an alternative sales channel you must first understand your customers' buying process. If most of your sales today are occurring over the internet then there is no need to create a channel of independent sales agents or manufacturers' representatives when the money could be better spent on search engine optimization and an e-commerce module for your website.

You need to determine how, when, where and why your customers buy your product or service. If most of your competitors are selling through retail operations then you may need to find one wholesale organization that currently sells to your target market and form a partnership with them. If you sell computer accessories then an e-store and a computer wholesaler may be all you need to bring your product to market. If you support the reseller and e-store with good marketing, PR and advertising programs then you may have the foundation for your channel.

If your product or service has a high value or a complicated buying cycle then using well trained sales people may be the only method to reach your target customers. The advantage of turning this type of sale over to an independent sales agent instead of using your own direct sales force usually hinges on two issues. First, the cost of establishing a direct sales force in many areas, especially if you do not have local representation, can be very high. Secondly, the use of an agent who already has either an established brand in the territory or contacts in your target market can allow you to quickly reach your potential customers. We will go into these topics in more detail in the next chapter when we discuss the many different alternate sales channel models currently in use.

How Much Can I Save by Outsourcing My Sales Operation?

This is probably the most frequently asked question I hear, when a company is looking to institute a channel of independent sales agents. All too often business owners see this move as a cost cutting measure instead of a method of generating more revenue, especially in territories or markets where they have little or no representation.

I see this as an accounting question (how do we cut costs?) instead of a sales question (how do we increase revenue?) If you are looking at utilizing sales agents as a method of cutting costs then you are most likely not going to dedicate the money and resources you will need to make the channel successful.

A sales agent channel needs administrative support, a sales management structure, and support from accounting, production, shipping, legal and most other divisions within the company. The training and management of your sales agents will require a dedicated structure which will cost money. The amount you need for the budget will depend on how serious you are about making the channel successful. Low budget commitments will usually produce low budget results.

Are you pitching a tent or building a structure you want to endure? Too many business people that are looking for sales agents are taking what I consider a "pup tent" approach to the exercise. They want to buy a cheap tent but expect it to perform like a well-constructed building. You can't approach the sales channel in this manner. If you are not willing to spend money to build a lasting structure then you are bound to fail right from the start. Your sales agent program needs proper planning, a strong foundation, framework, the right materials and internal systems to keep it functioning. This must all be overseen by a qualified manager to keep the project on track. If you build a sales agent channel with the same process it will have a much greater chance of success.

Before you determine whether a sales agent program is right for you, you need to determine whether your customers will buy from agents and if this type of sales channel makes sense. The first step in this process is to determine where and how your current customers buy.

Who Are Your Customers?

In order for you to find out who might buy from you in the future, you need to know the common characteristics of the people or companies that have bought from you or your direct competitors in the past. When you understand this information, you have begun the process to define where you should focus your selling efforts. This is very important because it will help you determine the best sales channel to reach your target customer.

The key to defining your target market is to identify these similarities so you can find other companies which share them. This is where you will want to target your prospecting and marketing activities since they provide the greatest opportunity for business.

The most important point to remember is that you need to have a clear focus for your sales agents. You can't afford to have them wasting time prospecting in areas where they will never find customers. If you can't define your target market clearly you will have a hard time finding someone to represent your products. Most established sales agents focus on very specific markets and call on specific accounts and they won't want to work with you if you can't show them exactly who your prospects are and what tactic should be used to begin a conversation with the prospect.

Coaching Exercise 1 - Identify Your Target Market by Segments

To begin the process list all the products or services you want to sell through a network of sales agents. This doesn't need to include all the components of each product or service you sell; it should just be a general listing.

If you have multiple lines then create a second ranking based on the profitability or the market share for each of the products.

	Products/Services	Ranking
1.		
2.		
3.		
4.		
5.		
6.		
7.		
8.		
9.		
10.		

Now you need to list your target customers for the products or services. Based on sales history, competitive information, industry knowledge or any other quantifiable business intelligence, create a list of prospective buyers. Here again you need to rank which buyers are your best potential customers.

	Target Market	Ranking
1.		
2.		
3.		
4.		
5.		
6.		
7.		
8.		
9.		
10.		

Example – Widgets Are Us

Products/Services	Ranking
1. Water-proof widgets	A
2. Shock-resistant widgets	D
3. Truck-mounted widgets	B
4. Stainless Steel widgets	C
5.	
6.	
7.	
8.	
9.	
10.	

Target Market	Ranking
1. Marine Supply Companies (wholesale)	A
2. Trucking Industry (fleet of more than 10 trucks)	B
3. Shipping Companies (domestic 50 + employees)	C
4. Boat Builders (commercial 25+ employees)	D
5.	
6.	
7.	
8.	

Create a "Wish List" of companies you would like to have as clients.

1.
2.
3.
4.
5.
6.
7.
8.
9.
10.
11.
12.
13.
14.
15.

Sales Agent or 100% Commission Sales Person

What is the difference between a sales person who is compensated on a 100% commission program and an independent sales agent?

This is a very common question and there are a number of specific differences. When we discuss commission-only sales people we are referring to a sales person who works directly for a company and is only paid a commission based on the sales they close. This type of sales person is found in real estate, the copier industry, door-to-door sales, financial planning, insurance sales and many other industries. They often work directly for a company and are considered by legal definition as employees. This means they would have all the advantages of working for a company. This may include company benefits, withholding tax, retirement or pension funds, vacation pay and the ability to progress within the organization.

On the other hand, the term *sales agent,* or *independent sales agent* (ISA) as used in this book, signifies an independent business person. Sales agents have connections with specific markets, industries, or product lines and they may represent one or more companies within their business model however they are never considered employees of the company.

From a legal perspective sales agents are independent from the company or products they represent. In fact, if their relationship is not seen as completely independent then there is the possibility in the eyes of the law that the company could be responsible for them as if they were a direct employee. This is why it is very important to have proper contracts with your sales agents that lay out the relationship details so there is no misunderstanding in the future.

You should always consult with a lawyer when you create your sales agent agreement to ensure it is worded properly to clearly define the "independent contractor" relationship between the company and the sales agent or sales agency.

Red Flag: Always consult with a lawyer when you are creating an agreement with contractors or independent sales people to ensure they are not legally considered employees.

Should I Consider an Independent Sales Agent?

Answering this question is a very important first step and will help you avoid making mistakes in your sales and marketing strategy from the start. I am regularly approached by business people who want to hire sales agents because they have been told it's a low cost model for getting their products in front of buyers. Unfortunately I see two common problems with this type of thinking. First, the company may not have any knowledge of the alternate channel business and they are just going to jump in and hope for the best. The second problem is that sales agents either don't exist or are few and far between in many markets and industries. If you don't know where agents fit into the current market you can spend a lot of time and money searching for business partners in an industry they don't service.

In an article by Hans Peter Bech, *Steps to Designing and Executing Productive Partner Channel Programs in the Software Industry,* Peter states; "the bad news is that your people's experience and skill-set and your organizational processes are not designed or geared towards building and serving a channel. The bad news is probably also that your product is not designed with a partner channel in mind either. Changing from direct to indirect sales requires that you change your business model and maybe even your product."

Before you decide whether you should try and recruit sales agents you must determine how and where people traditionally buy your product or service. If you have a new product then you will need to conduct your own market research to figure this out. Knowing how your customers buy is a major step towards determining if it is appropriate to use a channel of sales agents.

On the other hand, if you conduct your research and determine that there are already sales agents in the field then you may determine it's safe to proceed. Another question to consider is whether your business can support a single sales agent or multiple agents? If you have always sold through a direct sales force, an online store or a catalogue then you may not have the right structure in place to work with sales agents. Many business owners with the best of intentions have failed because they were unable to train and support external sales agents.

According to information form the Research Institute of America, between 50 and 80 percent of manufacturers use independent sales representatives.

Are There Sales Agents in My Industry?

A quick way to determine if sale agents are available in your market is to use one of the free database search tools available from companies like the Manufacturers' Agents National Association, www.MANAonline.org or RepHunter, www.RepHunter.net. Both of these companies allow you to conduct searches of their databases using keywords to find out if there are existing agents. You can search by product line, territory, customer profile, key contacts and just about any other key words that are important to your search. The great thing about most of these searchable databases is you only pay when you actually request an agent's contact information.

Here is a list of some of the most common industries and markets where you will find independent sales agents. This list is by no means comprehensive and you should research your specific industry to find out more about opportunities for working with agents.

Industries Where Independent Sales Agents Are Usually Found

Agriculture	Manufacturing Products & Services
Apparel	Medical Devices
Arts, Crafts, Gifts	Mining – Products & Equipment
Automobile	Nutrition
Books & Media	Office Supplies & Equipment
Business Consulting & Business Services	Packaging Products & Equipment
Consumer Electronics	Printing – Commercial Services & Equipment
Computer Hardware & Software	Publishing & Advertising
Construction	Real Estate
Decorating	Retail
Educational Products	Security Products & Services
Electronics	Sports, Leisure & Fitness (Services & Products)
Energy	Telecommunications
Finance/Investment	Textiles
Food & Beverage	Trade Industry – Plumbing, Heating,
Health, Beauty, Cosmetics	Construction Products, Tools etc.
Industrial Products & Supply	Transportation & Logistics
Internet	Toys
Jewelry, Eyewear	Utilities
Machinery	Wholesale
Marketing & Advertising Services	Web & Application Development

The second question you need to ask is what are the objectives of your sales agent channel? Companies create alternate sales channels for a number of reasons. The following is a sampling of some of the most common channel objectives.

- Provide representation in a territory or marketplace where they currently have little or no representation, visibility or sales
- The company does not want to establish a directly controlled sales or distribution structure for selling to end users
- The cost of sales using a direct sales force is very high
- Channel partners are independent therefore no employee benefits, no need to hire more sales and support people – reduced overhead
- The go-to-market process can be faster than hiring and training direct sales people
- Company may have no expertise in the market they are entering
- Company may not have the budget to expand the direct sales channel
- The company is looking for affiliates to promote the product and generate leads

Whatever your goal in creating an alternate channel, it is important to align it with the goals of the potential business partners. A sales agent that believes you are just looking for a cheap sales channel and thinks you are not prepared to invest in the long term development of the structure and relationship will not be interested in your program.

If your retail customer is content to purchase and download software online, then you don't need 100 stores reselling your software package. The money earmarked to establish a sales agent program would be better spent driving brand awareness and traffic to your website. On the other hand, if the product has a high value and is very technical in nature, you may need a trained representative who can understand the client's needs and show them the benefits of the product as it applies to their specific situation.

Looking Beyond the Financial Picture

A company which has historically used a direct sales channel to sell its products or services often fails when they institute a sales agent channel strategy in an effort to grow their customer base. This move, while well intentioned, often has disastrous results for both the organization and the would-be sales channel partners.

The problem is most companies can easily grasp the financial requirements of a new sales channel such as pricing and the promise of a lower cost of sale but they fail to consider the way the program will impact all other areas of the relationship with the sales agent and the end user. While you may have considered the formal structure which includes contracts, price books and territory assignments, a comprehensive channel structure must also include a complete action plan which will be your road map to manage and develop the relationship over the long term.

When you create an alternate sales channel you must remember you now have two customers for your organization: your sales agents who become your business partners and the consumer who is the ultimate customer. Unfortunately, as is often the case with the organization looking to establish the new channel, they attempt to sell to both the sales agent and end user with the same sales messages and business strategy. This will not work.

To build a successful sales agent channel you must always remember you will need a new business model incorporating both the management of the channel and the management of the customer process. Don't try and attract agents by using a sales strategy when you actually need a clearly defined recruiting strategy.

The following is an excerpt from my interview with Karen L. Jefferson, CPMR, CSP, and Executive Director of the Manufacturers' Representatives Education Research Foundation (MRERF) based in Denver, Colorado. MRERF is a charitable education foundation sponsored by manufacturers' representatives associations in diverse industries. In our interview Karen brought up a number of very important points that will help companies that are considering using sales agents.

What is your advice for companies that have never worked with sales agents?
Karen: *"Before approaching a prospective rep, manufacturers need to understand what reps do. They need to talk to other manufacturers that use reps or attend MRERF's Manufacturer's Best Practices. The function of reps is not widely known."*

What challenges does MRERF have when working with a manufacturer?
Karen: *"The biggest challenge is awareness. Awareness of the rep function and how cost-effective it is. Awareness of our programs that help build these crucial relationships. We have resources that can really help them."*

Do you see the rep business as a growth area?
Karen: *"Yes, I see a real opportunity for more reps to expand their businesses. There are reps in every industry and while industries will come and go, there will always be sales."* Karen also noted that more organizations, such as select international trade commissions are looking to develop relationships and work with reps in the U.S.

What advantages do you find when a manufacturer starts working with sales agents?
Karen: *"Sales agents are often into accounts that a direct salesperson could not or would not penetrate. Because of their synergistic line card, they are already selling other products to these customers. Now they can show them new products and solutions. This is a big plus, in addition to sharing the cost of sales with other manufacturers."*

What role does MRERF play in assisting the sales agents business?
Karen: *"MRERF offers a number of training programs for both the sales agents and the owners of multi-line sales agencies. They can study and receive their CSP (Certified Sales Professional) or CPMR (Certified Professional Manufacturers Representative) designation. When manufacturers partner with CPMR and CSP graduates they are working with agents that are committed to improvement and excellence. The goal of CPMR is to teach rep owners to move from reactive to proactive in their business."*

What are some of the problems that your members have experienced when working with manufacturers that are new to the sales agent channel?
Karen: *"The companies don't have a plan and are not prepared to give the rep enough time to develop their business. The attitude is often 'read the booklet, take the quiz and get out and sell'. Additionally, manufacturers sometimes play their cards close to the vest causing reps to guess what is happening. Trust one another. And pay commissions on time."*

www.MRERF.org

Benefit of Independent Sales Agents

Working with independent sales agents instead of full time direct sales people has a number of benefits for your company. Here is a list of the most common reasons companies establish alternate sales channels using agents.

- Fixed costs: No salary, limited travel costs, no benefits – commission on sales.

- Existing relationship: Agents know your target market and should be connected to the contacts you are trying to reach. Consider how long it will take a direct sales person working for your company to develop the same relationship the agent may already have in the territory and marketplace you don't currently cover?

- Tenure: Studies show that the average sales person will only stay with an employer for two years before they begin to look for a new job. Sales agents have usually made a lifetime commitment to the industry.

- Industry and territory knowledge: An agent can help the manufacturer by understanding the local economy because of their local knowledge. These reps can also provide valuable feedback on competition and product changes.

- Sell or starve: Agents only make money when they are selling. They historically work more hours, earn larger incomes and don't waste time on non-productive sales activities.

- Piggy back effect: A direct sales person who does not have a relationship with a company must develop trust before they can begin the sale. An experienced agent already has the relationship and when they meet an existing client they can introduce your product easily while discussing other lines they already sell to the customer.

- Lower cost of sale: It costs a manufacturer or principal less to sell to consumers using sales agents rather than a direct sales force.

- Greater marketplace coverage: A company can quickly expand into new territory.

On the flip side, when you are working with sales agents you have to be willing to give up control and be prepared to take action if your agents do not give the attention you expect to your product or service. When they are in front of their customer they are in the driver's seat and their success with your product and their relationship with you will determine how much of their selling time your product is going to receive. Help them make more money and they will bend over backwards to get your product into their customers' hands.

Companies often contact me to discuss whether a customer will be more receptive to a local sales agent or a direct sales person. In most cases the answer is in favour of the sales agent. If the agent is located in the same city or region as the customer then they should have an advantage over the direct sales person who must travel into the territory to sell their products then periodically make a return trip weeks or even months later.

Sales Leads: Many companies employ a comprehensive marketing strategy and then fail to follow up with the customer when the time is right. It is critical that you employ a proper **CRM (Customer Relationship Management** program) to track and initiate follow-up contacts.

All too often a customer is ready to purchase only to have a busy sales person fail to contact them in a timely manner. Days or weeks later when the sales person finally contacts the prospect they discover the potential customer has either gone cold because another crisis has taken center stage or they have purchased a competitive product. The sales person inevitably reports back that it was a poor lead and a complete waste of time.

For more information visit www.b2bsalesconnections.com

Don't Underestimate A Sales Agents Local Business Connections!

Not too long ago I worked with a client that had closed its offices in many of their smaller markets. Under a new strategy they would send sales people on a regular basis from the head office to visit the customers and fill their orders. This worked for a short while until a competitor began to use the company's absence in the area as a tool to boost its own sales by letting the local business community know that local jobs had been lost at the price of corporate profits. They also pointed out that the company was now just swooping in and selling products without any regard for the welfare of the community.

The local customers quickly came to resent the tactics of the absent manufacturer and started switching over to the competitor's products. Sales plummeted and the territory soon lost its best accounts to the competition.

In order to fight back the manufacturer re-established local sales agents in each territory and began to promote the fact they were back in town and utilizing local business people as their partners. A customer could now buy from the parents of the children their kids were playing soccer or baseball with, who attended the same schools, church and are part of local community groups. With this new direction not only did the company turn around their fortune, they ended up growing the new sales agent division to a more profitable level than it was when they employed local sales people who were only in town long enough to learn the business and then transfer to the major centers.

Sales agents can open doors and make introductions in many cases to prospects and customers you would never meet using your direct sales team. A good sales agent is already calling on your target customer and may have been doing it for years before you came along.

Indirectly Controlled Alternate Sales Channels

This overview of directly controlled sales channels is included to provide you with a brief introduction to their place in the sales process. The purpose of this book, however, is to focus on selling through an indirectly controlled alternate sales channel utilizing independent sales agents or manufacturers' representatives. Although telemarketers and outsourced sales organizations are alternate sales channels, they are usually hired for a short time frame and paid a fee based on hourly rates, leads generated or sales completed. They also charge fees for the design and implementation of the program before it goes into effect so be sure to understand the full costs of their services in advance.

Indirectly controlled alternate sales channels, which for the sake of simplicity will be called *Alternate Sales Channels,* have their own unique characteristics. The key difference is these are companies or individuals who will be entering into a long term agreement to represent your products or services in an effort to grow both your business and theirs.

The alternate channel partner is not an employee of your company and they are only paid when they sell your product or service. This type of partnership requires a full channel program strategy to create, launch, maintain and grow the win-win relationship.

Examples of this type of Alternate Channel Partner include:

- Retail stores selling directly to consumers
- Distributors/Wholesaler
- Value Added Resellers (VAR)
- Resellers or Dealers
- Independent Manufacturers' Representatives
- Independent Sales Agents

Retail: This is often the last step in the distribution chain for products designated for the consumer marketplace. The product may go from a manufacturer to a distributor and then a retailer before it reaches the consumer. Each business at each step in the process adds their markup to the price in order to make a profit. In the case of large retailers such as Walmart™ or Costco™ they can be the wholesaler, distributor and retailer in one.

Distributors/Wholesalers: This type of channel makes bulk purchases from a manufacturer and then resells the products to smaller customers in the distribution chain such as retailers. They rely on volume movement of products to make their profit. As with the retail example, they may also have a retail division which sells directly to consumers or businesses.

Wholesalers are often the link between you, the manufacturer of the product, and the end user. They have established channels to move products and allow you to take advantage of their operations and logistics. The drawback for small companies is large wholesalers and distributors often dictate the price a manufacturer can charge instead of the other way around. One of the dangers of this is when a manufacturer becomes reliant on a single distributor only to lose their entire sales channel if their product is bumped by a competitor's entry into the system.

Value Added Resellers: VARs are primarily found in the technology industry but are also used in other industries. Typically a VAR is looking for products or services which complement each other and can be combined into a single package as a way to 'add value' to their sales process.

When I was selling for a business technology VAR, we would purchase printers, computers, electronic weigh scales and proprietary software to build a shipping manifest system. The combined value of the hardware was only a few thousand dollars. However, when we combined the hardware, software and our expertise into a manifest system, it had the potential to save large volume shippers tens of thousands of dollars each year. Using this value added process we could sell the equipment for many times the actual price of the individual components. The sum of the whole had a far greater value to a customer than the price of each part.

VAR's will also represent other products that complement an existing product or service even if it does not allow for a large profit margin. Often these products are seen as lost leaders to keep the customer loyal to their company. A VAR that sells computer systems may also sell paper, toner, office supplies and other products that have low profit margins to insure a steady stream of purchases and in an effort to remain top of the customer's mind.

Resellers or Dealers: In many industries or markets, companies would establish independent dealers instead of a direct sales force to sell their products. Dealers would be legally independent of the company much like a franchise owner. The dealers would buy their products directly from the manufacturer and provide dedicated territory coverage. Over time more and more dealers moved to complete independence from their supply chain as they responded to changes in technology and customer demand in the marketplace. Today many large companies are acquiring independent dealers that are in their market in order to recapture a share of local customers.

An example of this is the photocopier industry. Throughout the 1990's and continuing today, large copier companies have acquired independent copier dealers and merged them into their business model to recapture market share.

Independent Manufacturer's Representatives: The manufacturer's sales rep historically represents only one manufacturer and may cover a large geographical territory. The product may be very specialized and the client base very small making it easy for one sales person to cover a state, province, or even an entire country.

Entrepreneur Magazine considers this sales person the "graduate level of selling, offering potentially higher earnings and freedom from company politics." Many companies' use this type of sales channel because it is considered one of the most efficient and cost-effective ways to sell high value products. If the manufacturer's representative is an employee of the company then they are considered a direct sales rep not an independent manufacturer's representative.

Independent Sales Agents: Unlike the independent manufacturer's rep, the independent sales agent is a self-employed commission-only sales person. He or she will represent as many product lines as they consider profitable and manageable. The sales agent will primarily have a specific market where they focus their attention.

Depending on the individual sales agent, some may only represent one product or manufacturer, whereas others may represent a dozen or more products that complement each other within a specific marketplace. Often, there are terms in their contracts which will not allow them to carry any products which are considered "competitive" to the manufacturer's own product line or the agreement may even restrict them from selling the manufacturer's full product line.

Companies such as Xerox™ have aggressively developed sales agent programs in outlying territories to compete with independent copier companies that are prevalent in most small to mid-sized markets. This program has been very successful in recapturing market share which was being eroded by the local dealers.

Three Simple Models for Sales Agent Programs

As a business owner or manufacturer you have the opportunity to develop any type of sales agent model you can envision as long as it is feasible for your business. Whatever you do, try to keep it simple. The more complex you make the program; the more difficult it will be for potential partners to understand the value to them.

I have provided a brief outline of three of the most common models in use. The first one, authorized company sales agent, is by far the most common structure. The second one, affiliate lead generator, relies on the agent to develop leads within their target market and then pass the pre-qualified lead along to the company. This concept is gaining in popularity as more and more companies and industries are looking to develop "affiliate" programs as a way of increasing sales.

The final agent model is the of the sales agent reseller. This model is more costly for the agent and exposes them to a greater level of risk and reward. Independent agents resellers purchase products from their suppliers and then resell them to their customers.

- **Authorized Company Sales Agent:** In this model the customer always belongs to the manufacturer or principal not the agent. The independent sales agent sells a product to the end user but most often the administrative work and service responsibility is handled by the manufacturer and payment is made directly to them not the agent. At the end of the month or commission cycle the manufacturer calculates the total sales for the agent and pays them a commission based on the agent's sales volume.

In this model the agent benefits by not having to invest in startup costs, inventory or take on any service responsibilities. They are independent sales representatives but are most likely under exclusive contract to sell for only one manufacturer or principal. The company retains full control of all the sales, marketing and distribution of the product and retains the ownership of the ultimate customer. The sales agent does not purchase or acquire title to the products. They strictly find people who are going to purchase the product from the manufacturer or principal. The downfall for the dedicated company sales agent is the inability to build lasting value in their business model. The company can cancel their contract and the agent can be left with nothing.

Independent sales agents are often a very good sales channel since they have established clients and a foothold in a territory or marketplace where a company would like to expand. The downfall for the manufacturer or principal can often be that same independence. Independent agents sell what they want and often won't commit to your product if a new and better opportunity presents itself.

- **Affiliate Sales Agents – Lead Generators:** In this program the agent is primarily focused on developing leads for the manufacturer or principal and once the lead has been prequalified it is turned over to the company. This type of relationship allows the agent to focus on lead generation and then move on to the next opportunity quickly. It can be a win-win for both partners when the program is working.

I have worked with a number of companies that had an internal sales structure which could handle more business but they were not able to provide the market penetration they needed to develop additional leads. Using sales agents as lead generators, they were able to quickly expand their marketing efforts at a very low cost and reach a large number of prequalified prospects.

Unlike the dedicated sales agent who develops the lead, meets with a prospect, provides a quote and closes the sale, the affiliate sales agent's only task is to find and pre-qualify leads. They are paid commission only when the company secures the business with the prospect.

This type of program can be very lucrative for both the company and the sales agent. The agent identifies a prospect, carries out a preliminary fact find to determine if the prospect is a valid opportunity and then turns the information over to the company. The company in turn will connect with the prospect, develop a proposal and finalize the sale.

A disadvantage of this system for the sales agent is that the program may not be structured to create a recurring revenue stream. If the agent develops the lead and passes it along to the company then any future sales may not be credited to the sales agent. If the company wants to keep their sales agents engaged and looking for additional opportunities within a customer then they would be wise to create a recurring revenue stream. Sharing the profit will go a long way toward keeping the sales agent motivated.

Consider a commission structure with a specific payout for new accounts and a lower payout for repeat business. A percentage of commission can be used to drive a hunting style lead generation program for new business while the agent farms their existing accounts. We will cover the commission program in more detail later in the book.

- **Independent Reseller Agent:** In this model the sales agent purchases products from the supplier at a wholesale cost and then resells the product to the end user at the retail price.

Here the agent keeps the difference between the retail selling price and the dealer cost price as profit margin. Using this business model the customer would be purchasing directly from the independent sales agent's own company, not the supplier. In many cases the manufacturer never has any contact or knowledge of the end user and the relationship with the customer is controlled by the sales agent.

A sales agent that is reselling a company's product must be prepared to invest in inventory, storage facilities, shipping operations, accounting, service support and all other parts of the business operation. This model requires a complete support infrastructure. The agency would be responsible for hiring and training both the service personnel and administrative staff necessary to run the business. The benefit is usually a larger profit margin on each sale because the agent has made more of a commitment to the manufacturer.

In many industries there are large sales agencies that represent multiple product lines within a complementary marketplace. These multi-rep agencies often have sales agents working directly for them across a larger territory or an entire nation. It's not uncommon to find agencies in both Canada and the United States that employ dozens of sales agents. Some of the larger firms have sales professionals spread around the world. If you can find a multi-rep agency to work with it can quickly give you even larger target market penetration.

Now that you have investigated the various types of alternate sales channels you can begin to develop your go-to-market strategy. The focus of this training manual will be on using independent agents as your business partners. In some instances you may use one specific agent and in other areas you may find you will need to develop partnerships with a few different companies. For the purpose of this book the term sales agent will include all the fore-mentioned types of sales channels. Although there are specific differences between these unique channel structures most of the sales process will remain the same.

As you can clearly see, there are many different types of sales channels available. Your goal should be to find the channel or channels which best serve the needs of your company and the buying habits of your customers.

Interview with Craig Lindsay CSP, CPMR, President, Pacesetter Sales & Associates
They are Canadian independent manufacturer's representatives providing quality "value-added" service for a select group of principals in the safety and industrial sectors. Their objective is to provide successful sales/marketing initiatives that reach the desired goals of all parties (principal, distributor and end-user).

When a manufacturer or principal approaches you, what do you look for in a potential business partner?

Craig – *"I want to see if they have done their homework. Do they understand my business model? Have they contacted companies that I currently represent and found out more about what we do? Have they contacted my customers or principals to find out about our relationship? When I investigate a new line I want to make sure the principal is committed to the program and is not going to provide a short term focus."*

How do companies usually approach you?

Craig – *"We are well known in our industry and marketplace so most often they know we sell for either competitive or complementary companies. Most simply pick up the phone or send me an initial email asking to discuss the opportunity."*

What are some of the poor approaches you have seen over the years?

Craig – *"I am always surprised when a company comes right out and wants us to sell their product line without knowing anything other than that we are in the same market they are trying to penetrate. They don't know me, we have never met, yet they are ready to offer us their product based on what they have 'heard'."*

What advice would you give a principal looking to establish an agent program?

Craig – *"If you want control of your sales process, hire a direct sales person, not an agent. Too many companies expect to control the agent's activities. It won't happen. You have to get your head around this being a partnership. Agents can open doors for you. With margins shrinking and costs increasing sales agents make sense for more and more businesses."*

What type of reports do you provide to your principals and why?

Craig – *"I represent 10-12 different companies at any given time. This means it is impossible to do individual custom reports in the format that each supplier would like. Instead we use the CRM program SalesForce.com. We send the companies a monthly opportunity report that provides accurate information on our activities. We also copy the company contact person on most of the emails we send to customers so they know what's happening. They will often review the emails and send us comments to help advance the sales process."*

Do you see the use of sales agents increasing or decreasing in the future?

Craig- *"More and more large companies are finding their direct sales force is a huge expense. Cost of sales is rising and the ramp up time for a new sales person can take months or more. Sales agents already have the relationship in the territory and can often take your product to market in weeks not months. With agents getting paid on results it really makes sense for companies to consider this sales channel."*

www.pacesettersales.com

How Much Will It Cost to Recruit a Sales Agent?

The first question that is most often asked by company executives looking to establish a sales agent channel is, "how much will it cost?" The answer should be based on the projected sales for the territory. How much revenue do you expect to generate from a specific territory? Once you have this projection you can begin to formulate a plan of attack based on your budget. Since an independent sales agent partner does not cost you salary, benefits or expenses, your upfront costs will be similar to recruiting a direct sales person. On the other hand, the long term benefits will be a reduced cost of sale for your company.

If you are currently selling your product or service through a direct sales force then you should be able to project the potential income of the agent's territory based on current sales figures. If you are introducing a new product or just starting out then you will need to create a sales projection in order to determine your costs and profits.

The book **OUTSOURCING THE SALES FUNCTION** by Erin Anderson and Bob Trinkle is a great place to start if you need to research the cost of a direct sales force as compared to an outsourced program. This book provides a detailed analysis comparing the cost of direct sales people and the cost of operating an outsourced sales team.

If you employ a direct sales person to cover a new territory it often takes a substantial investment of time and money before the sales person is producing consistent, significant results. Sometimes months of selling time are invested along with tens of thousands of dollars in salary, travel, and other expenses.

If you team up with a sales agent who is from your industry and already has contacts in your target market then you can reduce the ramp up time and costs substantially. Utilizing sales agents who do not get paid if they don't sell can be a cost effective way to establish a new territory. After all, sales agents only get paid on results whereas a direct sales person most often gets paid regardless of their sales performance.

Using low cost or free recruiting services may never prove successful. If you have a specific timeline for hiring sales agents then you will need an active search program.

The Cost Benefit of Independent Sales Agents

One quick way to determine the cost advantage of using sales agents is to compare their costs against the costs of a full time direct sales person. Taking into account expenses, benefits, overhead and all the other fixed costs you would incur for a direct sales person, there is often a sizable advantage when comparing the cost of selling through an agent.

Example

Direct Sales Rep			Independent Agent	
Annual Sales	$1,000,000		Annual Sales	$1,000,000
Fixed Salary	$45,000		Sales Comp @5%	$50,000
Commission @4%	$40,000		Fixed Salary	$ 0
Benefits	$7,500		Benefits	$ 0
Overhead	$1,600		Overhead	$ 0
Expenses @3%	$2,400		Expenses	$ 0
Total Cost	$96,500.		Total Cost	$50,000
Cost of Sale = 9.65%			Cost of Sale = 5%	

The example above is based on a 5% sales agent commission. The commission will vary depending on your industry and the profit margin of your products.

Another way to examine your cost of sale is to calculate the hourly wage you would have to pay a full time sales person. To do this you need to take the rep's targeted total sales for the year and divide it by 2,000. (The average person works 2,000 hours per year). Since most sales people spend less than 25% of their time actually selling, you need to multiply this hourly rate by 4 to calculate the cost per hour selling. The rest of the time is spent on travelling, meetings, paperwork, administration and other non-selling activities.

Annual Quota	Hourly Cost	Selling Cost Per Hour
$250,000	$125	$500
$500,000	$250	$1,000
$750,000	$375	$1,500
$1,000,000	$500	$2,000

It doesn't matter how you look at the numbers, the cost of employing a sales person is very high and you need to consider this when comparing the advantages of a direct sales force with those of using independent sales agents. If your direct sales force only costs you $125 per hour you are still paying that rate whether they sell or not. On the other hand, you only pay an agent when a sale is made.

Why Sales Agent Programs Fail

The success of your sales agent channel will be determined by many different components: recruiting process, training programs, program management and your support structure to name a few. Alternate sales channels usually fail because of one or more of the following problems.

- Lack of planning and support from the company
- Lack of commitment from the agents
- Lack of communication between the company and the agents
- Conflict between your direct sales people and the agents

This relates back to what we reviewed earlier in the chapter. It's a typical problem: companies looking for sales agents do not plan much beyond the recruiting process. If potential agents do not see a clear plan of action from you then they are going to be lukewarm or not interested at all in the opportunity. On the other hand if you have a clearly defined structure then they will be able to see the benefits of representing your product and will be more likely to engage in the process.

Over the years I have frequently seen a failure to plan for and support a new sales channel as the cause of the new program falling apart right from the start. The company often believes they are ready to work with an independent sales agent partner only to discover they do not have the sales processes and tools they will need to run the program. If you don't have marketing material, training material, price books, catalogues and a comprehensive step-by-step selling process ready to go, the agent will quickly abandon your product line and move on to other suppliers or go back to tried and true products.

Another reason for failure is caused by the conflict that develops between your existing sales channels and your new one. This most often occurs between your sales agents and your direct sales force, when they become rivals in the same sales territory or vertical market. When this happens the agent will most likely abandon the relationship. This is a business partnership with both parties looking for a win-win relationship. If you are trying to squeeze every possible dollar out of a territory by having your own channels competing amongst each other for business you may end up losing the agents commitment. Competition is healthy but too much internal competition will work against you.

Sometimes a lack of focus or commitment on the part of the sales agent is the reason for the programs failure. Many agents believe more is better and take on too many products and try to cover too much territory. This leads to cherry picking the accounts and only selling products that pay the best commission. This in turn results in the agent failing to service other accounts properly. It comes back to the 80-20 rule. 80% of your sales revenue will come from just 20% of your products and customers. You need to work with agents who can focus.

Another common problem occurs when manufacturers appoint a sales agent and provide them with limited resources and expect them to sell and communicate back to the manufacturer on a periodic basis. This is a mistake. Never assume the agent will communicate with you unless they have a problem or have made a sale. As the company sales manager you are responsible for the performance of a sales agent network, and part of that responsibility to set up frequent communications with them. Your communication plan should include regular emails, phone calls, webinars and product training.

In chapter 5 there are a number of ideas and recommendations for remote communication with your sales agent channel. You may have the greatest ideas and plans in the world but if you don't communicate them to your channel partners they may feel abandoned. Remember the old saying: "*If you don't take care of your customers your competitors will.*" The number one reason cited for leaving a current business partner and moving to a new supplier is 'perceived indifference.' If you are not actively engaging your sales agents then you are leaving them open to defect to your competition or abandon your products completely.

When this happens you have lost more than your sales partner, you have created a new competitor with precise knowledge of your pricing structure, your marketing plans, your product features and benefits, and possibly damaging competitive information. Yes, you can attempt to prevent this from happening with a non-disclosure or non-compete agreement but they are not always effective tools for protecting your information and trade secrets.

Finally watch out for part-time sales agents. They may try and convince you they have the time, expertise and contacts in your industry but they are not working their business consistently. They may have other businesses operating or be retired and looking to keep selling as a way of paying for vacations, toys or to supplement their income. If you are looking to build your business and improve your market and territory penetration you can't afford to team up with people who are not ready to attack the challenge full time.

"Great principals understand how the rep model works. They understand that nothing is free, take a collaborative approach to working with reps and make it easy for the rep team to work with them. Great principals are responsive, they get quotes and sample requests back to the rep in hours instead of days and reps don't have to ask or follow up two or three times.

They provide great training insight. Great principals share information and have reports that arrive timely and are complete. Great principals understand that reps make an investment of their time and money in a line and do the same in support of the sales channel. When that occurs it creates an environment that makes it easy for a rep team to be successful, which will win the principal more share of mind."

Tom Walker - N6TVZ Excerpt from a LinkedIn discussion – Feb 2013

"I have been active in the rep business both as a manufacturer's rep and as a national sales manager recruiting reps nationwide. In my experience, the formula is relatively simple. Reps want to rep companies and products that provide collaborative support and partnership that will compliment (sic) their efforts at representing your interests. The companies that do this the best will get and hold onto the best reps and rep groups. One way to think of it is this; if the rep has to do everything on their own they will eventually ask themselves why they don't just buy the product from you directly and redistribute it themselves? Or they'll wonder if their time isn't better spent with a company providing more support."

David Lane - General Manager at A1A Management LLC
Excerpt from a LinkedIn discussion on Manufacturers.rep – Feb 2013

Coaching Exercise 2 – Determine Your Sales Channel

1. Determine what type of channel you are going to use

    a. _____

2. List the objectives of the channel

    a. _____
    b. _____

3. List where your customers currently buy your type of products

    a. _____
    b. _____
    c. _____
    d. _____

4. List the 3 best ways to reach your potential customers

    a. _____
    b. _____
    c. _____

5. List sales agents in this market currently selling competitive or non-competitive products

    a. _____
    b. _____
    c. _____
    d. _____
    e. _____
    f. _____

Immediate Action Items

Have you completed all of the following?

- ☐ Identified who your customers are
- ☐ Completed Coaching Exercise #1 – Identify Your Target Market By Segments
- ☐ Checked free online sources to see if sales agents are in your market
- ☐ Listed the benefits of using sales agents in my company
- ☐ Determined if sales agents are going to be
  - ○ Authorized company sales agent (exclusive to our company)
  - ○ Independent manufacturer's representative (selling other companies' products)
  - ○ Lead generation sales agents (we make the sale)
- ☐ Ranked the profitability of your products or services
- ☐ Determined what products/services will be available through sales agents
- ☐ Identified your target markets, the market size or potential for the territories
- ☐ Determined the coverage model you will be using
- ☐ Determined whether to have exclusive or non-exclusive sales agents
- ☐ Created a plan for agents that want to sell your products online
- ☐ Listed all the companies who sell in this territory/market
- ☐ Created a target list of potential business partners
- ☐ Created a list of target geographic or vertical markets which will be a priority

Three most important concepts I learned in this chapter

1. _____

2. _____

3. _____

Chapter 3 – Components of a Successful Sales Agent Program

In this chapter we are going to investigate the components that make up a successful sales agent program so you can understand how to design a program for your company. Your goal should be to generate more sales for your business and expand into new territories so you can sell to more customers. According to many studies, 'lack of sales' is the biggest challenge facing businesses today. If you want to increase sales then these steps will help you create an agent program that can help you succeed.

> *"If you don't know where you are going, any road will get you there" - Lewis Carroll*

To accomplish this we are going to answer the following questions.

- How do I define my market?
- What is my "ideal" sales agent profile?
- How do I determine "what's in it for them"?
- What do I need to create a compensation program?

Start with Realistic Numbers, Not the 30,000 Foot View

If you have ever watched the TV shows *Shark Tank*™ or *Dragons Den*™ then you will have heard the potential investors crying out, 'show me the sales.' All too often the entrepreneur appears before the Dragons to pitch his or her product and fails in their attempt to woo them with grand statements of profits. The wannabe business people tell the panel of rich and powerful investor's tales of multi-million dollar market potential and their plans to capture a huge slice of revenue by only penetrating a fraction of the market.

The Dragons always respond the same way: "how many units have you sold and how are you going to use our money to help you sell more?" If the entrepreneur cannot answer these two simple questions they are shot down quickly and the product pitch dies.

As a manufacturer or principal selling your opportunity to a potential sales agent you need to adhere to the same sound business principals. Forget the fact you have millions of dollars in potential customer sales and focus on your current sales numbers. Your task is to answer the question "how will a sales agent be able to follow your business model and make money?"

If you think a sales agent will be able to sell 100 units per month but no one in your company has ever accomplished that sales volume then you are not being realistic. You need to have a concrete plan of action that will guide the sales agent through prospecting, appointment setting, fact finds, proposals, closing, delivery and installation stages in a step-by-step format.

Every day thousands of people all across North America attend "get rich quick" presentations. They are sold on the joy and financial freedom that comes from selling the next great product or service.

Many people invest thousands of dollars in multi-level marketing inventory that ends up sitting in their garage or basement. The only one to get rich and happy is the person who sold them the "bill of goods."

Your role as the channel principal or manufacturing organization is to create a viable business opportunity that a sales agent can use to grow their business and yours. To do this you must show them the benefits of becoming your business partner. I know it's a cliché but this relationship must be a win-win-win; a win for your customer, a win for your sales agent and a win for of you.

Size of Market: Sales Potential or Number of Potential Buyers

When identifying your target market you need to consider whether this is a business to business (B2B) or business to consumer (B2C) sales process. For example, if you are selling paper for copiers you may identify both markets as potentials for your products. But upon further investigation based on your selling price, location and current clientele, you may discover your plan to target the consumer market is not feasible. Likewise if you are selling cell phones you may determine that your best customers are people who walk into a retail store when they are looking to buy.

Whether you are selling B2B or B2C there are many ways of determining potential customers. Government departments provide free access to all types of research on consumer purchasing habits, demographics, geographic statistics, census figures and just about any other information you may require. The same applies to businesses. You can search by SIC code (standard industrial classification), the North American Industry Classification System (NAICS) listings and just about any other statistics you can imagine. The key is to determine what information is needed to create accurate forecasts, data maps and territories.

> *It is important that you create a clearly defined target market definition for both your sales agents as well as your customers. If you cannot provide your potential partners with a clear understanding of who buys your products it will be next to impossible for them to effectively engage the right people in their selling process. Please be sure to complete Coaching Exercise 1 – Identify Your Target Market.*

Once you have determined who can buy your products and what similarities they share you can move on to how you propose to divide the territory between your company and your sales agents.

What if I Don't Have Sales Yet?

In my conversations with sales agents there are two distinct camps on this topic. There are the larger multi-rep agencies that focus on working with companies that have full product lines and there are other independent agents who will consider a single product if they feel it has a very good market potential for them. Craig Lindsay, the President of Pacesetter Sales Inc., a multi-rep agency, said, *"I cannot afford to dedicate my time to pioneering a new product when I have commitments to my main product lines."* However he went on to say, *"If someone was an independent agent and saw a unique opportunity with a single SKU product they may take advantage of it."* You will face a much greater challenge attracting sales agents if you can't show them a proven marketing strategy. Expecting them to start from scratch and do "pioneering or missionary work" will not be easy and you may be asked to pay an up-front fee or retainer as they provide you with "feet on the street" during your start up stage.

If you are not familiar with the terms 'pioneering' or 'missionary' work in the sales field, it refers to taking an unknown product that does not have brand recognition and attempting to build sales in a new territory or market.

Most of the agents I have talked to agree that often a retainer is the only way to entice an established sales agent to do the pioneering work that will be required. If this is the case and you don't have a budget for paying a retainer then you may want to offer a higher commission on initial orders to help repay the agent for the extra work involved in a new product launch. Always be clear with the agents on exactly how much advertising and lead generation you will be carrying out in their territory to support them.

Territory Coverage Model

When determining how you are going to increase your exposure in a specific marketplace or industry you need to consider how you intend to segment the market. Here are five common methods used to segregate your market for the sales agents:

- Geographic Coverage Model
- Vertical Market Coverage Model
- Named Accounts
- Product Representation Model
- Mixed Coverage Model

Geographic Coverage: This is the most basic and easiest coverage model for a new sales channel. You determine where you would like your products to be sold and then assign each channel partner a territory based on their location. Depending on your market analysis you may determine for a high value product which has a very small prospect base to work with a single sales agent in a very large geographic territory. Your territory breakdown can be based on postal codes or zip codes, states or provinces or any other geographic designation. It is important to remember you need to be consistent and ready to enforce your rules if a sales agent is trying to sell outside their assigned territory.

For example, consider a printing equipment sales agent selling $100,000 printing presses. Your market research shows you a potential of 10-20 units per year in one province or state. Based on this information it may make the most sense to have one highly trained agent to represent you in their assigned territory.

In a second example consider an independent sales agent selling $500 IT solutions. Your market research shows that every business owner who has a website is a prospect for the product. You analyze the market and discover there are 10,000 prospects in one major centre. You may determine an agent can only sell in a very small geographically defined territory such as a segment of the city or specific zip codes. This way you can appoint multiple sales agents to properly cover the territory.

Whichever method you use to design your geographical coverage, it is important to consider the need to keep the territory as small and focused as economically feasible. If the territory is too large the agent may "cherry pick" the easy customers and not prospect for the customers that require more work. This can have a negative impact on your ability to achieve proper market penetration and sales volume. On the flip side, you do not want a territory so small that the agent has trouble identifying prospects for the products. If this happens they may decide to abandon your product and move to one that offers better opportunities.

Vertical Market Coverage: Another popular model is to have a sales agent selling into specific vertical markets. Using NAICS codes or SIC codes you can identify companies by name or common characteristics which you will assign your partners to contact.

For example you may be selling CRM software. Using vertical market coverage you reach an agreement with a sales agent who only sells to car dealers. Using this model you would authorize them to market your product to anyone in the car industry but not to businesses outside of the auto marketplace. If a prospective insurance company is looking for a CRM system then the sale must be handled by your sales agent who is responsible for this market segment. This model can work very well if you find agents who are very focused on only a few specific target markets and are prepared to follow the rules.

Named Accounts Model: This is not the same concept as establishing "protected" house accounts which the sales agents are not allowed to contact. Using a program of named accounts, the agents are only allowed to work with those specific companies. This is an easy system to implement but by restricting the agents from calling on new accounts or offering the product to their existing customers you may be limiting your product penetration.

If you are looking for a master distributor within a territory then you may have your agent working with a handful of named accounts who sell your product into their specific target market. An example would be having a sales agent who only calls on Home Depot™. He would be responsible for all aspects of this account but he would not be allowed to sell your products to anyone else.

Product Representation Model: Sometimes a product line may require very specific levels of expertise or selling skills. A business technology sales agent may sell small to mid-sized multifunction printers. However, the manufacturer may market a complex high end copier that requires a completely different level of product knowledge, buyer requirements and after-sale technical support.

The manufacturer may split the access to the product lines based on the specific product marketing requirements. Sales agent "**A**" can sell equipment up to a specific price and model and agent "**B**" can only sell machines of higher value or specific predefined model number. The manufacturer may even switch from an independent sales agent representing the lower value products to a direct sales person or independent manufacturer's representative for selling the complex high value products.

Mixing Channel Representation Models: It is very common for manufacturers that have extensive product lines and sell in multiple vertical markets within a country or region to have a mix of sales agents who have geographic territory assignments and then further breakdown the distribution channel by model or product lines.

K.I.S.S. – Keep it Simple Stupid: Whatever method you decide to use for your distribution and coverage model remember to keep the documentation simple and easy to understand. But most importantly make sure it is documented in your sales agent agreement with your channel partner so they clearly understand their position.

Finally, don't create one-off side agreements with your agents whenever you feel they are needed. This will destroy your credibility and hurt the channel over the long term. Be consistent and treat all your agents fairly.

Exclusive Territory or Exclusive Product Representation

I have followed many LinkedIn discussions over the years and you always hear agents arguing they must have the "exclusive rights" to a product. "If I can't be exclusive I won't sell your product." Don't be forced into making decisions based on these threats. If a sales agent requests the exclusive rights to sell your products, always proceed with caution. This may be a quick way for them to lock out competitors, including you, and then just hold the rights to your product until it's too late. By the time you are able to act you may have lost months if not years in sales opportunities.

If an agent approaches a manufacturer demanding exclusive representation in a territory then they need to be ready to undergo a detailed due diligence process showing you their business sales history and the sales targets that they are willing to commit to. You need to protect your business and they need to protect theirs.

A better approach is to discuss the opportunity you have identified in the territory and the strengths the prospective sales agent provides. Determine if you can negotiate an exclusive representation "time frame" where the agent must show you that they have the ability to sell your product. If an agent is looking for the exclusive rights to your product and you know the market potential is large then you can request they hire additional dedicated sales people. Another way to approach this request is to agree not to appoint another agent during a specific time frame, provided the agent in question meets the sales goals. This would give both parties an opportunity to assess the relationship and determine if it is a win-win.

Watch out for Exclusive Territory!

Always make sure you have a detailed cancellation clause in your sales agent agreement that will allow you to quickly renegotiate or cancel the agreement outright in the case of non-performance.

Coaching Exercise 3 – Sales Agent Opportunity

1. What are the products or services the agent will be representing?

    a. _____

    b. _____

    c. _____

2. Why is this product/service needed?

    a. _____

    b. _____

    c. _____

3. Who are your target markets or industries?

    a. _____

    b. _____

    c. _____

4. Why would a sales agent be interested in becoming your business partner?

    a. _____

    b. _____

    c. _____

5. Who is an ideal candidate to become a sales agent?

    a. _____

    b. _____

    c. _____

6. How will the sales agent benefit by becoming my business partner?

    a. _____

    b. _____

    c. _____

    d. _____

7. Who should a sales agent currently call on to make the most of this partnership?

   a. _____

   b. _____

   c. _____

   d. _____

   e. _____

8. What products does the agent currently sell that will be complemented by your line?

   a. _____

   b. _____

   c. _____

   d. _____

   e. _____

   f. _____

9. What challenges is the industry currently facing and how can you address them?

   a. _____

   b. _____

   c. _____

   d. _____

10. What is the compensation structure for the sales agent?

   a. _____

   b. _____

A sales agent that dedicates their time and energy to this product line could potentially earn $_____ per month and $_____ per year after a _____month period of education and training.

Using the space below write an opening statement that you would use to approach a sales agent and explain how becoming a business partner will benefit them.

_____

_____

_____

_____

Consider What a Sales Agent Is Thinking

When a company is considering an agent channel for their products and services I regularly ask them to conduct a brainstorming exercise. My goal is to get them thinking about the opportunity from a sales agent's perspective. Not only are you evaluating the sales agent, they are evaluating you, and if they are experienced in the business and you have never worked with sales agents before then you are not the one in the driver's seat.

On the following page I have included a list of potential questions that sales agents might consider asking to uncover more information about your business. Hopefully by reviewing the questions and considering your answers you will have a better understanding of their concerns and requirements. If there are questions on the list that you are not prepared to answer then you should have a well thought out justification for your reservation. You may simply want to state "it's too early in our discussion to address this specific issue but I will be happy to return to it at a later date."

I frequently conduct interviews with sales agents who have decided an opportunity was not right for them. Most often the company is very surprised to find out the agent isn't interested. When I talk to the agents the number one reason they cite for deciding not to proceed is the principal's apparent lack of direction and vision for the agent channel. This is especially prevalent in companies that have never worked with agents before. If an agent doesn't believe you have a clearly structured program then they are not going to be very interested in your opportunity.

> *"I have been active in the rep business both as a manufacturer's rep and as a national sales manager recruiting reps nationwide. In my experience, the formula is relatively simple. Reps want to rep companies and products that provide collaborative support and partnership that will complement their efforts at representing your interests. The companies that do this the best will get and hold onto the best reps and rep groups.*
>
> *One way to think of it is this; if the rep has to do everything on their own they will eventually ask themselves why don't they just buy the product from you directly and redistribute it themselves. Or they'll wonder if their time isn't better spent with a company providing more support."*
>
> **David Lane**, LinkedIn discussion December 2012, Manufacturers Representatives Group

Questions Agents May Be Asking You

1) Who buys the product and why?
   a. What problem does it solve for my customers?
   b. What benefit does it give me (the sales agent)?

2) Who are your primary customers or targets?
   a. Primary _____
   b. Secondary _____
   c. Tertiary _____
   d. Other _____

3) What is the territory?
   a. Why is it open?
   b. Was there an agent in this territory before?
   c. What happened to them?

4) Do you have a direct sales force?
   a. Where are they?
   b. Do we compete?
   c. How am I protected from conflict?

5) Do you use sales agents now for your business?
   a. Yes – how many do you have?
   b. No - Why are you establishing an agent channel?

6) What experience do you have partnering with sales agents?

7) Do you have other sales agents in place?
   a. Can I contact a few of them to get a feel for your company and the product?
   b. Do you have a sales agent council?
   c. What makes a successful sales agent?

8) Do you have sales for the product/service already?
   a. What are your sales volumes
      i. This year?
      ii. The last 3 years?

9) How do you determine a sales targets?
   a. Work with the agent and set goals?
   b. Assign a quota based on your corporate needs?

10) Is this product, market or service new/unique/growing/shrinking?

11) Do you have house accounts or protected accounts?
   a. What's your policy on adding new accounts?
   b. Are my accounts protected?

12) Do you have a sales agent contract/agreement?
   a. Does it contain a non-compete clause?

13) What is the commission structure for the product
   a. A new customer?
   b. A repeat customer?

14) Questions regarding commissions.
    a. When do you pay commissions?
        i. On shipment?
        ii. On payment of invoice?
        iii. What happens on back orders?

15) Do agents ever work together on sales?
    a. Do you have a policy for splitting commission?
    b. How do price discounts affect commission?
    c. What happens when a customer defaults on payment?
    d. Do you hold back commission?
        i. Why and when?
    e. Other _____

16) Questions concerning lead generation
    a. Are you generating leads for your agents?
    b. Do you have a specific marketing program in my territory?
    c. Do you offer marketing programs such as co-op marketing dollars for us to spend?

17) What is your warranty policy?

18) What is your delivery policy?

19) Who installs the product?
    a. Is there pre-delivery work for me to complete for installation?
    b. What type of work is it?

20) Are you selling online and is the price fixed for online sales?

21) Do you discount the product through other channels?
    a. If yes, what are your other channels?
    b. What is your discounting policy?

22) Do you have a printed or electronic price book?

23) Do you have a printed or electronic catalogue?

24) Do you have training material for agents?

25) Do you supply samples? If yes, are they...
    a. Free of charge?
    b. Paid for by the agent?

26) Do you have marketing brochures or other printed material?
    a. Who pays for shipping of marketing material?
    b. Who pays for shipping of samples?

27) Is the material available in electronic format?
28) Do you run marketing programs for the products?
    a. How often and what are they?

    b.   Social media
    c.   Direct mail, advertising, trade publications, online, pay per click

29) Do you have a co-op marketing program?

30) What type of training do you provide?
    a.   On site
    b.   At your location
    c.   Web-based

31) What sales tools do you have?
    a.   Training manuals
    b.   Email and communications sample templates
    c.   Proposal templates
    d.   Fact find documents
    e.   Objection handling scripts
    f.   Frequently asked questions

32) Do you attend trade shows?
    a.   Which ones?
    b.   What happens to the leads?
    c.   Do you offer incentives for agents to attend?
        i.   Full or partial expense reimbursement
        ii.   No expense assistance

33) Reporting and forecasting:
    a.   What do you require from an agent?
    b.   Are you prepared to work with our CRM report output?

34) How often can we expect a company representative to join us for field sales calls?

35) Do you own the patents or exclusive rights to the product?

36) Where are the products manufactured?
    a.   Do you qualify under the "buy American" designation?

37) Who are your competitors?
    a.   What is your competitive advantage?

38) Who will I be working with at your company?
    a.   Do you have a dedicated channel sales manager?
    b.   Do you have dedicated administrative or technical support for agents?

39) Why are you getting into the agent channel process?

40) Will you provide the contact information of a few customers for a reference check?

41) What is the start date for the new agent?

Be Prepared, Potential Sales Agents Will Be Judging You

You should be prepared for any or all of these questions from sales agents when you approach them for the first time. If you have never dealt with agents before and they are experienced then they will most likely have more questions for you than you will have for them. Preparation is the key. The more you know about what they may ask the better off you will be. By reviewing these questions you can prepare the information that may be necessary.

In my interview with Craig Lindsay, President of Pacesetter Sales Associates, he mentioned a couple of key points that are worth repeating here. Agents cannot provide a "magic wand" if your company is in trouble and sees this channel as a quick fix for poor growth. Working with agents requires a long term commitment in order to be successful. A company must do their homework and understand both their market and the agent's business model. Craig has 16 questions that he uses to determine whether his agency is going to proceed with new product or manufacturer. He rates the answers on a scale of 1 to 10 and if the company does not get a good grade they will decline the opportunity.

As an example, he will give a company a score of 10 if they currently use sales agents and a 1 or zero if he feels they are just experimenting with an agent channel. By rating the companies it saves him time and ensures everyone at Pacesetters follows the same procedures when they are evaluating potential partners.

If the good, experienced agent doesn't see a plan and structure in place they usually choose to pass on the program. If they aren't concerned then they may be inexperienced and not a good fit in the first place. As one agent said during an interview, "if you don't have a documented program in place then you'd better have a 'cure for cancer' otherwise I am going to walk." As Michael Greber author of the E-Myth Revisited states, "*in order for a business to work it must become a system so it works exactly the same way, every time, down to the last detail.*"

Show the agents you have a structure and system in place and you will be way ahead of other companies that are dabbling in the alternate channel program and just can't understand why agents are not interested in their products or services.

Determine Your Ideal Sales Agent Profile

Who is your ideal business partner? Is it a single independent sales agent or a multi rep agency that has a team of sales people and covers a wide geographic area? It is important that you create a profile of your ideal sales agent before you start your search.

In this chapter we have provided a sample *Sales Agent Fact Find* document which will help you determine if the candidate is a good fit for your organization. Before you concentrate on the characteristics of the individual business partner, you need to determine how you are going to find these potential sales agents and to do that you will need a sales agent profile.

One of the easiest ways to construct a profile is by looking at how your competition sells. If they have an agent program, then it may be a simple matter of investigating the characteristics of their partners. If we go back to our example of a copier manufacturing company then they would most likely target small office equipment dealers. They could also target sales people who are currently selling for a competitor or an independent business equipment dealer and offer them an opportunity to start their own business as a sales agent. This has been a very successful method in the business equipment world.

On the other hand, if you are in an industry that has never relied on sales agents then approaching sales people who are currently employees of a competitor may not be a viable solution. You may find someone who is looking for an opportunity to start their own business but does not have the investment capital required. As a sales agent they can enjoy the freedom of being their own boss without the capital cost outlay most often needed to start their own business.

Components of the Sales Agent Profile

Regardless of your target you will need to create a Sales Agent Profile before you start the recruiting process. This should include the following:

- What specific territory do they cover?
- How much industry experience do they have?
- What type of companies make up their existing account base
- How do they call on? (purchasing, C-Level, managers)
- Current marketplace; where they focus their sales efforts?
- What is their risk tolerance? (new agents)
- Do they have the ability to take on new products? (established agents)
- What is their current product line? (complementary and competitive)
- What is the size of agent's business? (sales volume and other staff)
- Are they willing to provide reference?
- Are they prepared to do "pioneering work" on new products?
- What is the corporate structure?
- Have they ever had legal disputes with other manufacturers?

Coaching Exercise 4 – Determine the Ideal Agent Profile

Here is a sample of the information you need to consider before you begin your agent search. This profile sheet can be modified so it includes all the information you determine necessary. When searching for agents I recommend you create a 'must have list' and a 'would like to have list.' This gives you a good starting point for the exercise.

Sales Agent Profile

Name of Agent: _____ Phone: _____

Email: _____

Products currently sold:
- Complementary
- Competitive
- Other _____

Industry focus:_____

Territory covered:_____

Customers they call on:
- Industry specific
- Vertical Markets
- Retail
- Wholesale
- Other _____

Level of contact they work with:
- C-Level, Owners
- Plant Manager
- Purchasing Department
- Other _____

Service capabilities – if needed:
- Area of expertise or training _____
- Type of certification required _____

Installation capabilities – if needed:
- Type of certification required _____

Years in Business:_____

Single agent or multi rep business? _____

Other selection criteria:
- a) _____
- b) _____
- c) _____
- d) _____

In chapter 4 – Recruiting Sales Agents, there is a check list of information you need to clarify before you enter into an agreement with a business partner. Partnering with an agent should be approached the same level of care as if you were hiring an employee. Before you agree to let a new agent represent your products or services be sure to conduct your due diligence, including extensive reference checks including customers and suppliers.

By now you have determined your market, identified your primary customers, started to map out your territory structure and decided on a sales agent profile. All that remains is to recruit the channel partners and start selling. Right! Unfortunately, with many companies that fail in the channel design process this is exactly where the planning ends and the old adage of "making it up as you go along" kicks in.

Now is the critical time for you to create the "recipe book" so you are following a detailed plan of action. We call it your **Sales Agent Playbook** and it should include everything an agent will need to know in order to sell your product, work with your company and become successful. If you start the recruiting process before the playbook is ready you risk the possibility of losing a good agent before they ever make their first sale.

> *"They (manufacturers) often poorly invest in the programs and do not know how to work with agents. ... Established agents can usually open doors that a direct sales force may spend months or years trying to get through. They don't understand what we can bring to the table and often don't value the relationship?"*
>
> **Dane Lawrence, President, Salesforce 1 (Independent Sales Agency)**

Before anything else, preparation is the key to success. Alexander Graham Bell

Create Your Unique Value Proposition – Twice

I am frequently asked to provide feedback on marketing material that companies intend to send out to potential sales agents. All too often this material is completely focused on the end user who is going to buy and use the product, not the sales agent. This type of marketing completely fails to address *"what's in it for me"* from the agent's perspective. You must remember that sales agents are not buying the benefit of the product; they are buying the benefit of being able to sell the product and the advantage of being your business partner.

Most companies succeed at defining what their product or service does for the end user but fail to clearly market the benefits of becoming a sales agent. You must step back and determine how your unique value proposition can be repurposed from their perspective.

To do this properly you need to identify all the ways your products or service can help your potential sales agent business. Here are some of the most common justifications that you should consider.

My product/service:

- Results in a lower cost for something that is equivalent to their current offering
- Provides a better result at the same cost
- Provides a unique solution to their problems/needs at a premium cost
- Helps them acquire new customers or sell more to their existing customers
- Is innovative and helps set them apart from their competitors

Given that the ultimate goal of a business is to make a profit, any product or service you are selling must be perceived as helping the sales agent make more profit, either by increasing revenue or by reducing expenses. To do this you must create a compelling marketing message that will show potential sales agents how they can increase their sales and improve their customer service by becoming a business partner with you.

"It is all about support and providing a value add to the rep organization. It is up to the principal to provide leads, follow-up, work closely with the rep to ensure success on sales growth and new design activity. I have seen too many times that the principal expects the rep organization to do it all. This is not the 'real world' as reps have had to add more lines to remain whole and it is a team effort to increase sales. I have always been the principal managing reps and I give rep organizations a high 5. I have seen a few rep organizations that do not make the effort but those are not the majority. It takes time, effort and support from both sides to make this work."

Sandy C, January 2013,
LinkedIn discussion, Manufacturers' Representatives Group

What Is a Sales Agent Partner Looking for?

An **Entrepreneur** magazine study reported that *"82% of businesses want to increase their revenues."* When approaching agents you need to consider how your opportunity is going to help them grow. Here are a few ways that your products or services could help a sales agent build their business.

- New products or services to enhance their current offering
- Increasing penetration within existing customer accounts
- Opportunities to get them in the door of new accounts – differentiation
- Providing recurring revenue streams
- Exclusive territory
- Sales and service support from the manufacturer or principal
- Sales and service accreditation
- Authorized Manufacturers Representative Program
- Marketing support, advertising programs, co-op marketing funds
- Brand awareness
- Lead generation
- Protection from sales conflict

As you create your sales agent information kit keep this information handy. It will help you design your initial contact materials using language that the agents are interested in hearing. The better you understand what they are looking for the easier it will be to get a conversation going with them.

Once you have connected with a prospective sales agent you need to begin an in-depth interview process to determine if they are the right fit. You should create a sales agent interview fact find sheet and a score card to benchmark their strengths and weaknesses against other prospective agents. Often we have seen companies accept an offer from the first sales agent they find only to spend time and money trying to get out of the arrangement shortly after the relationship starts.

As you interview the agents they should also be assessing you to determine whether the opportunity is a good fit for them. As you conduct your fact find they should be conducting one on you. Reviewing the document provided at the end of the chapter, *Questions Sales Agents Need to Ask When Considering a New Partner,* is one of the best ways for an agent to ensure they are covering all the bases. Some agents may have more thorough than others, but you should be prepared for either. If an agent does not ask you questions about your opportunity then you need to be concerned because they are most likely inexperienced and haven't thought the relationship through. If the agent does have questions, then you don't want to be caught unprepared.

Conduct Your Own Market Research: Often the easiest way to determine who can sell your product and to identify the reasons why they would be interested in selling your product is to find a few prospective sales agents and contact them directly. Pick up the phone and call them and ask about the products they currently sell and what challenges they have experienced. Once you have some background information ask the agent directly what they look for from suppliers when they are considering representing a new product.

Another way to conduct your market research that is fast and inexpensive is to ask questions using LinkedIn groups that focus on your target market. There are a number of very good sales agent groups that are open for anyone to join. It's also a great way to start a conversation and meet potential agents.

Once you have determined from your research why an agent would benefit by becoming a business partner you will need to create a value statement that outlines "what's in it for them" before you make your initial contact.

The book **Why People Don't Buy Things** (Washburn & Wallace, 1999) explores a number of studies on buyer psychology. Here are what they consider the five most powerful arguments for change:

1. Hidden risks revealed
2. Hassle-free alternatives
3. Raising expectations
4. Fear of being outdated or left behind
5. Do it right so you don't have to do it over.

The exercise on the next page will help you create your unique selling proposition for your product or service. If you can't answer any of the questions from a sales agent's point of view then call a few agents and conduct your own market research. Your goal is to create a succinct statement that will quickly get them thinking, "this may be for me?" Your goal is not to sign them up as a sales agent, it's simply to get them talking to you about the opportunity. Don't jump into selling them on your product; you just want to get a conversation going at this point.

See the attached *Sample Sales Agent Profile Research Questionnaire*. This document will provide you with a series of questions you can ask a potential sales agent to determine how they assess new products and business partners. You can modify this for your specific requirements.

Coaching Exercise 5 – Determine Your Unique Value Proposition

1) Who is currently your primary target market?

    a. _____

    b. _____

    c. _____

    d. _____

2) What are your prospects' problems – (bigger the pain = better the gain).

    a. _____

    b. _____

    c. _____

    d. _____

3) What solutions do you provide for their problems?

    a. _____

    b. _____

    c. _____

    d. _____

4) List the quantifiable results that you can deliver ($$, %, time).

    a. _____

    b. _____

    c. _____

    d. _____

5) Explain what makes you different – be brief and to the point.

    a. _____

    b. _____

    c. _____

    d. _____

6) Determine the 5 most important points identified in 1 – 5.

    a. _____

    b. _____

    c. _____

    d. _____

7) Your goal is to answer the question, why should a sales agent do business with you?

_____

_____

_____

8) My unique value proposition statement for a prospective sales agent is:

_____

_____

_____

_____

_____

9) Does this value statement clearly let them know the benefits and opportunities of your product offering from a business partner's point of view? What's in it for them?

_____

_____

_____

10) My statement of proof for a prospective agent is:

_____

_____

_____

11) Have I supported the value statement with a quantifiable statement of proof?

- Saves time or money – provide examples of money saved or actual time saved
- Solves a problem – case study of how you helped others
- Fills a need - prevented loss, injury, damage – how or what you did
- Increases revenue – productivity – brand awareness – etc.
- Creates a gain - leads to success by?

Fact Find for Prospective Sales Agents

Taking the time to properly interview and assess prospective agents is paramount to the success of your channel growth. Too many relationships start based on good "gut feelings" and end up a "train wreck" for both parties. The key is to conduct structured interviews and learn as much about your prospective partners as you can before you commit pen to paper in a formal agreement. The best partnership is a Win-Win-Win.

Once you have determined who you are going to contact and how you are going to approach them, you need to be ready to quickly move from the initial interest stage to the structured assessment of their business and how well it fits with your model.

When you are contacting the agent for the first time you need to have a very simple fact find to determine whether they are a qualified lead or not. Neither you nor the agent has time to waste if the opportunity is not a fit. With this in mind you should be able to ask a few initial questions to find out if an opportunity to move forward exists. It is just as important to disqualify an agent when you are prospecting as it is to qualify them.

The initial fact find should only include the basic information you need to determine if the agent is a candidate for you.

- What territory do they cover?
- What other products/services do they currently sell?
- Are they a competitor?
- Do they call on prospects at the right level in an organization?
- Do they know about your product/service?
- Do they have the time and the resources to take on new products?
- What do they bring to the relationship?
- What type of technology do they utilize in their business?

Take a few minutes right now and outline a number of fact find questions that you would use to determine if a sales agent is a good candidate as a business partner.

1) _____

2) _____

3) _____

4) _____

5) _____

6) _____

7) _____

8) _____

We have included a sample sales agent fact find template and a sales agent score card template in this section. The fact find includes many of the questions you need to cover before you make a decision as to the suitability of the prospective agent. The sales agent score card lets you quickly compare the prospect against the requirements you have determined are needed in a sales agent. The second score card will help you quickly compare a number of individual sales agents against one another in case you have to determine the best fit in a territory where you have more than one good prospect.

Don't be afraid to reject a candidate if they are the only one you have found in a specific territory. You are better off to continue looking for a sales agent that is a good fit instead of accepting one that is not an ideal candidate. Getting it right the first time will save you a lot of frustration and anguish in the long term compared to hiring the wrong person and then have to fire and replace them.

If you have determined there are a number of potential partners in a specific territory then you will need to determine which one will be your best fit. To do this, assign a point scale to each area of your agent profile and determine if specific areas will be weighted with greater values than others. If you need a company with service capability for your product and one prospective agent has a large trained service group and the other prospect has little or no training then you would assign more points for the specific requirements they meet.

Verify the information with physical evidence in the form of sales reports, accounting documentation, service records or any other information you can accumulate when possible. The more you know about each prospective partner the better your possibility for success. Don't be afraid to call current customers to determine their level of customer satisfaction when interviewing a potential sales agent or manufacturer's representative.

> "If you don't know who the reps are that you want, then a good place to begin is by making inquiries to the buyers at your targeted customer list. Just come right out and ask them who is representing this or that product. And finally, you can get referrals directly from other reps and rep groups themselves. Reps are quite a nomadic bunch. It may be likely that a great rep just decided to become independent or open his/her own firm and is seeking new clients. This happens all the time and you should be ready to take advantage."
>
> **David Lane - Excerpt for a discussion on LinkedIn Manufacturers Representative Group, Feb 2013**

The following page contains a sample *Sales Agent Profile Fact Find* document. You can use this sample to create your own fact find and decide what particular information will be needed to determine if the prospective sales agent has what you are looking for.

Coaching Exercise 6 – Fact Find – Initial Contact

Product/Services Currently Represented	Notes

Sales Agent Contact Information	
Name:	
Address:	
City:	Prov/State:
PC/ZIP:	Web:
Phone:	Title:
Email:	Cell:
Years In Business:	Legal Status – Incorporated, Sole Proprietor, Partnership

Competitive Product/Services Represented	Notes

Vertical Market Focus	Notes
Primary Target Market – e.g. Fortune 500	
Secondary Market – e.g. Hospitals, Schools	
Other Markets Covered	

Primary Contact Level within the Market	Notes
C-Level, Owners	
Purchasing department only	
Plant or Facilities Manager	
Other	

Territory Covered	Notes

Continue to the next step in the recruiting program ☐ Yes ☐ No ☐ Undecided

The purpose of this initial fact find is to determine if the sales agent is a potential business partner and whether you should continue the discovery process.

Sample Sales Agent Fact Find Template- Detailed

Company Contact Information				
Company:				
Address:				
City:		Prov/State:		
PC/ZIP:		Web:		
Contact Name:		Title:		
Phone:		Cell:		
Email:				
Years In Business:				
Number of Locations:		Legal Status – Incorporated, Sole Proprietor, Partnership		

Product/Services Currently Represented	Sales	Service	Notes

Additional Information	Yes	No	Notes
Sales Agent has a physical location			
Boardroom/training room			
Demo Room			
Warehouse Facilities			
Service Department			
Website			
Ability to update website content on site			
Interactive website content – collect leads online			
Marketing staff			
Administrative staff			
Number of service people (if applicable)			
Trained service staff			

Vertical Market Focus	Revenue	Notes
Main Focus – (e.g. Fortune 500)	%	
Second Target – (e.g. Hospitals & Retirement homes)	%	
Third Target	%	
Other Targets	%	

Current Competitive Suppliers	Notes

Current Non-Competitive Suppliers	Notes

Key Factors	Excellent	Good	Not Acceptable
Overall management quality and stability			
Previous experience with supplier as a sales agent			
Vision for the company			
End-user value proposition			
Willingness to share business information			
Knowledgeable in key areas required			
Focus on target markets			
Certification in industry/market			
Overall growth prospects			
Service support systems if needed			
Budget for staff training			
Advertising and marketing budget			
Key account development			
Market share/penetration			
Customer satisfaction			
How do you monitor your sales process? CRM or other?			
Are you prepared to provide sales activity reports to us?			
Have you segmented/classified your territory by accounts?			

Description of geographic territory coverage:

_____

_____

_____

Do you develop an annual budget and marketing plan? Describe current one:

_____

_____

Have you ever been involved in a legal dispute with a supplier or a company you have represented? Describe:

_____

_____

What is your unique value proposition?

Sales Agent Suitability	Yes	No	Notes
Do you have any non-compete contracts in place?			
Is this agent suitable for the program?			
Continue to next phase?			

EXAMPLE: Assessing a Single Sales Agent Candidate

Here is a quick and easy to use sample template to determine the sales agent's suitability for your needs. By assigning a point value to attributes that either the agent must have or you would prefer that they have, you can quickly assess their strengths and weaknesses.

Key Requirements	Possible Point Total	Actual Point Value
Years in Business	10	8
Industry Experience & Knowledge	10	2
Ability to Represent Your Product	10	3
Annual Sales – Low, Good, Exceptional	10	2
Geographic Territory	10	4
Service Capability (if required)	10	1
Management Support	10	1
Current Customer Base	10	8
Industry Accreditation	10	2
Willingness to Provide Reports & Forecasts	10	10
Use of Technology to Monitor their Business	10	5
Total Points	**110 possible**	**46**

This table can be as comprehensive as needed in order to make informed decisions based on the information available. By using a point system and structured interviews with each prospect you will eliminate the need to rely on "gut feeling" and instead rely on data using a balanced score card for each agent.

The second example allows you to compare a number of potential sales agents quickly to determine which prospects are the best fits. This can be applied to all open territories or you can use it to select from a number of prospective sales agents who are competing in the same territory or marketplace to represent your product.

The key is to determine your requirements and then create a chart and point scale to weigh each of the requirements. The factors which are considered most important for success in this specific example have been highlighted. These will differ based on your specific needs.

> ⚠ Don't get caught in the mindset that more is better. Many small specialized niche sales organizations outsell the larger competitors who represent a multitude of product lines. Focus and dedication are often the best solution.

EXAMPLE – Assessing Multiple Sales Agent Candidates

Key Requirements	Possible Point Total	Prospect 1	Prospect 2	Prospect 3
Years in Business	10	8	9	9
Industry Experience & Knowledge	10	2	9	5
Ability to Represent Your Product	10	3	7	2
Annual Sales – Low, Good, Exceptional	10	2	7	3
Geographic Territory	10	4	7	5
Service Capability (if required)	10	1	8	5
Management Support	10	1	7	2
Current Customer Base	10	8	8	5
Industry Accreditation	10	2	5	5
Willingness to Provide Reports & Forecasts	10	10	10	1
Use of Technology to Monitor their Business	10	10	5	2
Total Points	**110 possible**	**51**	**82**	**47**

Survey Prospective Channel Partners: The purpose of the survey is to uncover what both you and the agent are looking for when determining what new products and partners to work with. Remember the key is for this to be a "win-win" relationship.

In the appendix is a *Sample Sales Agent Application Form*. This template will help you create your own form for interviewing potential agents. You can modify this form as required to create a document that covers all the information you will need to determine the suitability of a business partner. This is not a legal document. All forms should be reviewed by a lawyer before use.

How Many Sales Agents Can You Recruit?

Once you have determined the number of sales agents you require to cover your territory or marketplace you will need to determine how many you can recruit and train at one time.

Don't be fooled into thinking that you can easily manage as many new partners as you can recruit. The logistics of dealing with 1 or 2 new agents is quite different than trying to bring on a team of 5 to 10 agents. When I managed a team of 22 sales agents based across the country I had a channel sales manager and a marketing and sales administration person who provided support for the program. If you have 8 or more sales agents who are actively involved in selling your product then you will need a full time administrative person to ensure they have the support they need.

If you have never worked with an alternate sales channel in the past then you need to be ready for the usual growing pains. The purpose of this book is to help you anticipate many of the common problems that occur when you launch your new initiative and to prepare you for the challenges. The last thing you want to do is recruit a group of motivated sales agents and then have your program fail because you are not able to provide the support and training they need.

When you don't have a channel sales manager or at least an administrative person ready to support the new agents then you can quickly get in over your head. Think small to start and then add more agents as the program develops and you have a better understanding of the complexity of managing the agent network.

If you are planning to have your sales agents report to your company president or a senior executive then they need to set aside time in their schedule to work on the program. If they don't have time and an agent needs assistance it can be very destructive to the program. When an agent needs help, they need it immediately. If you need a day or two before you can get back to them you will have lost their focus and most likely they will abandon your product. It is better to have an administrative or marketing person who can return quick answers and provide support to the program than to have a senior person responsible who can't act quickly when needed.

> "Great principals are responsive, they get quotes and sample requests back to the rep in hours instead of days and reps don't have to ask 2 or 3 times before the principal follows up."
>
> **Independent Sales Agent**

The moral of the story is not to allow yourself to get spread too thin as you manage the channel. You need to have time to focus on your new business partners as they begin to work with your company. Failing to focus on the agents will result in the program falling apart before they make the first sale. Before you set up a sales agent program determine how much time you can actually spend administering and managing the program once it becomes operational.

Creating a Compensation Structure

How are you going to compensate your sales agents? A partial answer to this question is already provided by the type of channel structure you have designed.

If the sales agent is simply going to be paid a commission for leads they develop or sales they close then all you need to do is create a commission structure based on your profit margin. This is one of the simpler programs to design. You already have your selling price and your compensation program will be based on a commission for each sale. If the agent covers all their own expenses then you need to create a program that can provide adequate compensation to produce an income that makes it worthwhile for them to represent your product.

If your commission structure results in the sales agent earning a few hundred dollars per month and they have a lot of road blocks limiting their ability to make a sale, then you can be pretty sure they will abandon your product line very quickly. A sales agent who can make a good living selling your products and not have to deal with the aggravation of a manufacturer that makes it hard for them to succeed will be much more productive. Your goal is to make the sales process as seamless as possible for the agent. That will motivate them to continue to represent your company and your products as their business grows.

When you approach a sales agent you must keep projected sales numbers realistic and lay out a plan of action on how they can reach the forecast sales results.

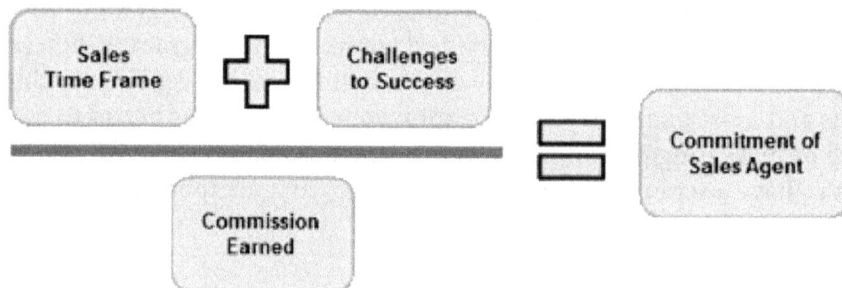

You should consider the figure above as a formula for sales agent productivity. If selling the product requires a long time frame and is filled with obstacles to making the sale then the potential return on the agent's work must be high. If the return is not equitable for them then they will not focus on your product. If, on the other hand, the time frame to close a sale is reasonable from the agent's perspective, and the challenges are not too daunting and the commission is good, you will get their focus. Think of it as their return on time invested (ROTI). The better the rate of return the more engaged the agent will be.

Commission and Bonuses

When working with 100% commission compensation structures consider an escalating payout scale that increases the commission to your agents based on sales volume or sales value. Keep the program simple to understand and easy to administer. If a sales person knows they make 10 percent on every sale up to $50,000 in a month and 15 percent on every dollar they earn in excess of the target then they can quickly calculate their profit and appreciate the goal.

Another example would be to pay 10% commission on all sales up to $50,000 and then a higher percentage on all sales during that period if they exceed the target. Now they not only make a higher percentage on their sales over the $50,000 target but they get more money upon reaching the target in the first place. It's up to you to determine what behaviour you want to drive with your specific compensation plan.

The most important point to remember is to keep the program simple and achievable. If no one in your organization has ever sold $50,000 in products in one month and the best sales people are only selling $30,000 monthly, then your agents will develop a "who cares" attitude and just sell what they can or worse still will focus their energy on selling products from the other companies they represent.

Another variable to consider is the commission payout on new accounts and repeat orders from existing accounts. If you are in an industry or marketplace where the customer will make regular repeat purchases once they have chosen you as a vendor, then you should consider creating a recurring revenue stream for your sales agent.

Share the Revenue: Frequently, companies will argue that recurring sales orders do not require an agent's involvement since the customer can just phone, fax, email or go on line and place their orders directly. They feel if the agent was not directly involved in the sale they do not need to pay them any commission. This is unfortunately a myopic view of the relationship between the agent and the customer and usually leads to a breakdown of the program. Cutting the sales agent out of these recurring sales can often backfire. If a problem occurs then there is no incentive for the sales agent to get involved and they may resent the fact that they established the account but are no longer being compensated. It is smarter to pay a lower commission on recurring revenue and keep the agent engaged than to cut them out of the process completely and create a problem. Remember, this is revenue you would never have earned in the first place if it was not for the sales agents involvement.

In my interviews with both agents and principals there is a real difference of opinion regarding the issue of repeat sales and recurring revenue streams. Sales agents are very clear in their viewpoint. "If you want us to sell your product then be prepared to compensate us on each and every order that originates in our territory, or from our accounts." In many cases this is a non-negotiable point when a company is working with a new sales agent doing pioneering work in the territory.

On the other hand, many companies are divided on this point. Some are more than willing to pay a commission on every sale in the territory including pre-existing accounts while others are not prepared to share anything more than they absolutely have to with the agent. A better approach is to pay commission on pre-existing accounts once the agent has been with the company for a specific period of time and is producing sales at their target quota. If you are going to take the position that they only get paid on the initial sales they generate then you will have trouble keeping your agents motivated and loyal to you.

If you are planning to split commission and house accounts with your agents then remember your compensation plan should be designed to reward this win-win scenario. If you pay a higher rate of commission for new accounts then it will help motivate your sales agents to always be on the lookout for new business. By paying for existing accounts you will be rewarding the agent for maintaining a strong relationship with your current customer base. You can easily set two different rates of commission if needed. One for new account and a lower rate for repeat business. However to structure the commission plan make sure it is reflective of your industry.

Recurring Revenue:

Commission on new account = X%

Commission on existing accounts = Y%

> Keep your compensation plans as simple as possible. If you need a complicated computer modeling program to calculate how your sales agents are paid or if your sales team is confused about how to calculate their own income, then your compensation plan is too complicated and you won't get the commitment you need.

One of the simplest formulas for figuring out the commission program is to pay a percentage of your profit margin to the agent. For example, if you sold your widgets for a total of $10,000, and those same widgets cost you $6,000 to produce, your gross profit is calculated to be $4,000. If your goal is to pay overall sales compensation at 20 percent of gross profit, that equates to 8% of your retail selling price.

B B SALES CONNECTIONS

Gross Profit Compensation Conversion Worksheet

Enter data in the yellow boxes to convert the overall amount of sales compensation to a percentage of sales.		
Desired Percentage of Gross Profit for Overall Sale Compensation		20.0%
Product Selling Price	$	10,000.00
Less Cost of Goods Sold	$	6,000.00
Gross Profit	$	4,000.00
Total Desired Sales Compensation	$	800.00
Desired Sales Compensation Percentage of Sales		8.0%

If you are not familiar with Excel, determine your sales compensation as a percentage of sales by dividing the total desired sales compensation by your total sales.

Sales Goals, Not Sales Quotas

As the business owner, should you set a quota for your sales agent or just leave the performance up to the individual? I am a firm believer in the need for written goals, targets and accountabilities for all sales people. If you read the advice provided by both Manufacturers' Agents National Association (MANA) and RepHunter® you will see that the preferred method is to work with your agents to develop sales goals, not assign quotas.

Instead of just setting a quota and expecting the agents to accept your imposed figures, you should have an annual meeting with the agent to discuss and agree upon a sales goal for the month, quarter and year.

You should also develop a plan of action that includes the specific objectives and accountabilities that you will both work toward during that time frame. Working together instead of mandating your objectives will let the agents commit to their performance. If they do not meet their goal then that should be part of your monthly discussion.

> To ensure your sales goal is achievable, divide the total target by your average size sale. This calculates the total number of sales required for the agent to reach their goal. If no one has ever sold the number of products required to reach the goal then adjustments need to be made. Remember, once your team believes they can reach their goals, they are halfway to making them happen.

During an interview, a former vice president of sales for a well-known technology company made the following observation when asked about the policy his company followed for setting goals or assigning quotas in his channel. He chuckled and said, "the company simply took the total sales they had forecast for the year, divided it by the number of divisions and you took what you were given – no discussion." While this type of quota setting is common the feedback from most sales agents who deal with small to mid-sized principals and manufacturers reflects the need for the annual targets to be determined by discussion and negotiation not mandate.

Today it is pretty much common knowledge that people are more likely to pursue goals that they determine are important to them. When goals or objectives are mandated by others the chance of the goal being adopted is much lower. After all when was the last time someone told you to lose 20 pounds and you immediately went on a diet.

How to Avoid Sales Agent Channel Conflict

Channel conflict can come arise from a number of different sources. Sometimes the sales agents compete with one another. Sometimes the agent competes with the company's direct sales force. Occasionally an agent will decide to sell your products online disregarding their assigned territory. Regardless of the cause of the conflict it is important for you to develop an agent channel conflict guideline or policy to deal with the problems as they occur. Better yet, ensure that you have clear policies regarding sales conflict in your sales agent agreement.

Channel Conflict Concerns

- Competition between your sales force and your agents
- Competition among agents
- Web-based sales into other territories
- Discounting to win business
- Price protection for one agent or channel over another
- Having a clearly defined process
- Unequal treatment when enforcing the rules

While a direct sales force may put up with internal problems that hamper their selling efforts, a sales agent will usually have a "three strikes you're out" philosophy. You can't afford to be disorganized or unprepared with your agents. They will drop your product line when they realize that dealing with your company is more hassle than it should be. They can also very quickly give your company a bad name in the industry and future sales agents will avoid you like the plague.

Another concern that follows closely with channel conflict happens when agents drop your product. While this is bound to happen from time to time as the agent's business changes or their focus on your product changes, you should be quick to determine if they are abandoning your program because of underlying problems you are not seeing. When an agent stops selling your product you should immediately place a call to them and find out what prompted the change. By acting quickly you may find there are issues you must address before the problem spreads to other agents in your channel.

I have put together a list that contains some of the most common reasons that agents stop working with a manufacturer. You should notice that most the problems are caused by internal issues that can lead to further damage if they are not addressed.

Reasons Sales Agents Abandon a Product or Supplier

- Discounting and heavy competition – can't make a decent commission
- Paperwork problems –errors delay fulfillment
- Shipping errors
- Commission not paid on time or disputes over commissions owed
- Poor inventory control – they made the sale but you are out of stock

- Product does not do what the customer was expecting
- Long sales cycles
- Low value product that require a high sales volume
- No feedback or poor communication
- Competing with the company's direct sales team or other agents

Lose Your Channel, Lose the Business

In the late 1990's a small US based manufacturing company signed an exclusive contract with one of the biggest players in the office technology market. They had offices in every major center and thousands of sales people across North American. The agreement looked like it was going to be a windfall for the manufacturer and overnight all the sales agents who had represented the company for years were told they could no longer sell the product. As you can imagine this lead to a loud outcry claiming unfair business practices which resulted in a number of law suits. The agents banded together and found a new product line to replace the one they had lost and redouble their efforts with the new product line.

A year later the nationwide distributor dropped the product line and the manufacturer went back to its former agents and tried to strike a new agreement with them. The agents had all committed time and money to the new product line and refused to work with the supplier. The following year the manufacturer company went bankrupt since they were never able to re-establish a sales channel for their products.

It may seem a little premature to address the issue of channel conflict at this point when you don't have a working sales channel, however, if you are prepared in advance for the inevitable event of conflicts between your company and your sales agents, then you will already be a step closer to the solution.

First of all, a certain amount of channel conflict is good. It indicates you have substantial market coverage when agents are experiencing overlap. If you don't have any conflict then you should look at ways to increase your market penetration. That could mean you need more sales agents within the territory.

When you design your territory coverage model you should account for possible conflict by setting up economic conditions and geographic limitations. Economic conditions are where one agent may receive a higher commission or bonus than another agent due to their higher sales volumes. You may also offer higher commissions if a sales agent is required to deliver, install or service your product. Geographic limitations are used to dictate exactly where a product may be sold by the agent.

Other methods to consider in eliminating or reducing conflict are the use of re-branding or only allowing specific business partners to represent portions of your product or service offering. Be sure to check with a lawyer if you are creating different pricing or commission structures within your program. You don't want to be breaking the law by creating unfair business practices.

Your goal should be to optimize market coverage and minimize channel conflict using a structured approach to the selling process. If you begin to see market erosion or a decline in the retail pricing of your product then you may be entering a period of destructive channel conflict or increased competitive activity. If this happens you should quickly discuss the symptoms with your sales agents to determine the cause. If the problem is channel conflict then you can take steps to address the underlying issues.

The bigger problem occurs when members of your agent channel begin to compete with either your direct sales efforts or other channel partners. Value quickly becomes lost as the parties aggressively compete with one another for the sale. If your agents begin to erode the profit margin to non-profitable levels in order to "buy the business" then you need to act immediately before it destroys the brand reputation and causes key agents to defect to other products.   Tread carefully in this area and consider consulting a lawyer to ensure you are not breaching any laws or regulations concerning your pricing policies.

When your price begins to drop and multiple agents are competing for the same account your customers will become confused and often will move to a competitive product to avoid the conflict.

Remember you need to create a policy document for conflict resolution, publish the policy to your partners and enforce the rules when conflict occurs. If the actions of your channel partners are corrected the first time a breach of policy happens there is less chance the problem will happen again. If it is a continual issue with an agent then you may want to re-examine their role as a business partner.

Promote Partnerships between Agents

Another way to minimize conflict between agents is to promote the use of partnerships. If one agent can offer a client a "turn-key solution" and another partner is only selling discounted "me too" solutions you may be able to connect the two agents and have them develop a relationship where they split the profit on a sale when they help each other generate new business.

Often companies will have inside (telephone sales) and outside sales staff paired up with each other to approach prospects in the same territory or market. If a contact centre sales rep uncovers a large opportunity within an account they will connect with the local sales agent and develop a dual account strategy.

When I was selling printing equipment we had an agreement in place with our agent channel. They were free to sell any product up to a specific model. When they encountered a prospect that needed a high production system they would introduce me to the client and I would take over the sales process.

Once the sale was made the agent would receive a portion of the profit plus the ongoing service revenue and supply revenue. By keeping the agent involved in the sales process and splitting the profit, the partner was quick to prospect for high value equipment and not try to sell the lower priced products that were not right for the customer application. This win-win relationship resulted in impressive market penetration in territories where we never expected to find customers.

Once the agent had assisted me a number times selling the production units we would train and certify them as authorized factory representatives who could now sell the equipment themselves. Many partners who began the relationship selling only a small segment of our product line quickly graduated to selling the high priced systems.

By controlling the sale of the production machines we eliminated the possibility of channel conflict, price erosion and customer confusion, and helped the agents develop much higher levels of product knowledge. We, in turn, strengthened our relationship with the partners and everyone enjoyed stronger profit margins and better market penetration. After all, isn't the whole purpose of your channel to increase market share in areas where you would otherwise not have sales?

Before you move on to the next chapter be sure to complete the action items at the end of this chapter. The goal of this book is to help you create a documented, repeatable alternate channel program as you follow along.

Immediate Action Items

Have you completed all of the following?

- ☐ Defined and created your territory coverage model
- ☐ Created your Unique Selling Proposition document
  - ○ For an end user of your product
  - ○ For your sales agent channel partners
- ☐ Completed reference checks on the potential sales agents
- ☐ Created a compensation plan for your sales agents
- ☐ Determined the target quota for each territory or prospective agent
- ☐ Assigned service support or technical support staff
- ☐ Addressed your internal corporate concerns
- ☐ Forecast the potential revenue for each territory
- ☐ Clearly determined responsibilities for each of the above requirements
- ☐ Created a timeline to accomplish the tasks
- ☐ Created a *Sales Agent Profile*

Three most important concepts I learned in this chapter:

1) _____

2) _____

3) _____

Chapter 4 – Recruiting Sales Agents

In this chapter we are going to focus on the agent search process. We will cover where to look, how to find them. We will also explore methods for connecting with agents, and information on creating a sales agent agreement.

Catching the attention of a sales agent can be a very difficult task unless they are actively looking for a new product line. Most agents easily fly under the radar which means using passive recruiting methods such as notices on your website, ads in trade publications or online job boards will be a complete waste of time. Consequently, active sales agent recruiting techniques, those where you target specific markets or territories, may be the only way you can attract sales agents.

"Look for people who will aim for the remarkable, who will not settle for the routine." - David Ogilvy

In our own practice we carefully review each recruiting program before we agree to work with a client. Our goal is to determine whether a potential client is in an industry or territory that is already serviced by sales agents or whether it is unlikely they will find one.

A passive recruiting campaign will take a lot of time and involve a substantial amount of marketing and PR work to get your company known. A combination of both active and passive recruiting techniques is always best with an active search campaign being front and centre. As much as most people don't like to make cold calls, it's still the fastest and best way to find and connect with a potential sales agent.

For most companies, searching for sales agents will be an uphill battle and very often the company will not be successful because their industry does not utilize the sales agent model. If this is the case then a direct sales force may be your only option. It is very important that you conduct some research before you commit your finances to the agent search process to avoid wasting money on a losing venture.

'We went through a lot of potential sales agents – when we first started we found the wrong people more often than the right people. Be prepared to spend a lot of time having to "hands on manage" the agents. Constant contact and follow up. Never assume anything. "When you find the right rep agency that has the experience and is prepared to run with it the process works brilliantly"

Greg Whittle – Body Guard Safety Products

Targeting Prospective Sales Agents

According to a study by *Media Matters,* in the 1970's a typical adult had the potential to receive over 600 ads on a daily basis. With the exponential increase in the use of technology that number has increased to over 3,000 ad exposures daily from all forms of media. Even if this number is off by 50% we still have the possibility to be exposed to over a 500,000 ads each year.

In addition the typical business person receives 50-60 emails per day and many people receive in excess of 100 daily. Now add text messages, social media, phone calls, meetings, interruptions and general time wasters and you have a whole lot of other things competing with your message.

Why is this important for your business? The reason is quite simple. When you are approaching a prospective customer or potential sales agent your message has to somehow break through the noise and confusion of the thousands of other messages. You have to find a way to capture their interest and move the prospect from their current attitude of "*whatever*" to a desire for them to say "*tell me more.*"

Sales agents, especially if they are successful, will be difficult to contact because they are busy people. You must be ready to make numerous phone calls and email contacts just to initiate the first discussion with an agent. When you finally reach that person you had better be ready to start a dialogue that quickly captures their interest. If they are well known in their industry and good at their job then they will be accustomed to constantly having companies approaching them. You need to stand out from the crowd when you get your chance.

A common mistake that most manufacturers or principals make when approaching prospective sales agents is to believe the person is only interested in their product or service. While the product is undoubtedly of value to the agent and their customer they are usually, and wisely, more interested in learning about your company as a business partner. What do you bring to the table? How are you going to help them grow their business? Your job is to convince them you are someone they will want to create a long term and profitable business relationship with.

Some of the key phrases agents are going to be interested in hearing:

- Exclusive territory, exclusive product or exclusive service
- No competition
- Niche market
- Above-average commission and recurring revenue stream
- In demand product or new product
- Innovative business opportunity
- Pre-existing account base
- Full training program
- Turnkey system

If you make any of these promises then you had better have the ability to back them up.

When approaching a sales agent you cannot rely on a marketing message that is targeted towards your customers to capture the interest of a prospective sales agent. You must also have a unique sales and marketing program that is specifically targeted at the agents. If you were Apple™ you could probably rely on a prospective channel partner to see your retail message and decide, "Wow, that's a product I want to sell." Unfortunately, very few companies can expect sales agents to be knocking down their doors wanting to represent them.

There are very few companies that have market domination like Apple™. Their fanatical customer loyalty has made them an exceptional case. When the latest version of the iPhone™ was scheduled for launch consumer electronics companies were lined up trying to obtain the rights to resell the product. The downside of representing 'in demand' consumer products is that the margins tend to be very low because of their market dominance.

The Apple™ example is a unique situation and for most companies the exact opposite holds true. A company can build the proverbial better mouse trap but without an aggressive marketing and sales campaign no one will ever know the product exists. If everyone is content with their old mouse trap and doesn't care there is a new one and if sales agents don't want to market an unknown and unproved product, then you have to create the consumer need for the product or you will fail.

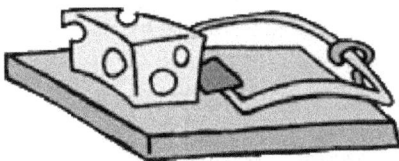

One of my favorite stories that brings this into perspective is the mousetrap itself. According to the US Patent Office over 4,000 patents have been filed for mousetraps but today the market is still dominated by the over 100 year-old technology of the spring loaded bar mousetrap.

A handful of others have been successful but the vast majority of "better mouse traps" never made their inventor a penny. Richard Maulsby, of the U.S. Patent & Trademark Office states there are over 1.5 million patents in effect in the US and only about 3,000 are commercially viable. He goes on to state that 99.8% of the patents fail to make money. There are a lot of companies out there building better products, unique products and innovative products but they still fail to make money.

> *If you want something new, you have to stop doing something old."*
> *— Peter F. Drucker*

Interview with Dane Lawrence, CSP, Owner SALESFORCE1.

Dane provides qualified sales and marketing personnel to take on business development roles for companies in transition. He minimizes the hiring risk through the understanding of outsourcing costs, so business owners can concentrate on other areas of their business.

As an independent sales agent, what do you look for when a company approaches you?
Dane – *"I am interested whenever a company comes to me with a unique product that could be a 'game changer." It has to have appeal into my target market and fit with my business model. I also have to be sure it will be financially rewarding. I'm also not interested in commodity products."*

How do you keep on top of new products your customers may be looking for?
Dane – *"I keep in close contact with my accounts and I am always asking what products may be subject to a category review. When I know a product or line of products is up for review I see this as an opportunity for me to help the customer with new products that they may be looking for. With my regular customers it's as simple as saying, 'tell me what you want and I will find it for you."*

When a new company approaches you what are your concerns?
Dane – *"I always consider the financial situation of the company. Will they be around in 6 months or a year? Do they pay on time? Do they have a plan?"*

What advice would you give to companies that are looking to establish a sales agent channel?
Dane – *"They have to realize that I have spent years building my reputation with my customers and if the manufacturer screws up they can destroy that reputation and my business. It's the agent who is at risk not the manufacturer if something goes wrong because we introduced the product based on our relationship with the customer."*

"They also need to have a 'roadmap for success' especially if you are expecting an agent to do pioneer work on new products. Too often they are poorly invested in the process. They have a 'here's your catalogue now go sell' approach."

There are some sales agents who argue that the only reporting they need to do is send in orders and provide phone updates once in a while. What is your policy on reporting to the company?
Dane – *"I meet with my principals to develop annual targets for both sales revenue and account penetration. I update the forecast 3 or 4 times per year and communicate regularly by phone and email. I also copy my contact inside the manufacturer on emails between my customers and me when it is appropriate. This way they know what's happening and often they are proactive with information to help me with the sale."*

Do you think companies view sales agents as a cheap alternative to a direct sales force?
Dane – *"Unfortunately, yes. They often poorly invest in the programs and do not know how to work with agents. If they want the control they have with a direct sales force then they need to hire a direct sales force. Established agents can usually open doors that a direct sales force may spend months or years trying to get through. They don't understand what we can bring to the table and often don't value the relationship."*

www.salesforce1.ca

What is the Cost of an Empty Sales Territory?

When determining how much you are going to spend to recruit either a sales person or a sales agent you should first determine how much it costs you to have an empty sales territory. Most often the expense of taking slow action or not spending the money on an effective recruiting program is far outweighed by the cost of no immediate action. After all, are you worried about the cost of the problem or the cost of the solution?

Leaving a territory vacant may seem like a good idea - after all not paying a sales agent is saving you money, right? But in reality, a vacant territory, especially one that previously was covered by a sales person or sales agent, is most likely costing you money. Not only are you losing revenue but you are also failing to properly support loyal customers and you are giving your competitors a free pass at your customer base.

Vacant Sales Territory Means:

- Loss of revenue
- Loss of market share
- Loss of brand awareness
- Wasted advertising and marketing dollars
- Competitors get a 'free pass' at your existing customers and new accounts
- Your customers may not be receiving the support they need or expect
- Customers will take the opportunity to shop around for a new supplier
- Your current sales team may be "cherry picking" deals within the open territory
- Your customer is frustrated because no one is working with them
- Your support structure for the territory is not following up on critical issues

The longer a sales territory is vacant the greater the cost to your company. On the other hand, if you have identified a new territory where you would like to sell your products or services then you need to consider the cost of delay as a lost opportunity for your business.

> *"Things may come to those who wait, but only the things left by those who hustle." ~ Abraham Lincoln*

Where to Find Independent Sales Agents

There are many places you can go to look for independent sales agents. You should start your search using websites and directories which are focused on your industry or marketplace. Most industries have their own trade associations that compile an annual membership directory. In some cases you can search the directory free of charge and in other instances you must be a member of the association to access the directory. Either way, this is one of the best places to begin.

If you need to go beyond the directory or if none exists for your specific market then you will need to widen your search. I have listed a number of options below. Remember these costs do not take into account the number of hours you will need to spend to research your industry, place ads, screen out junk mail and spam, and interview the prospective candidates. If this is undertaken by the business owner or your sales manager then you need to account not only for their time working on this project but also their loss of actual selling time and revenue.

Where to Find Sales Agents

Referrals	Free – if you can get them – often a slow process
Career Page on Your Website	Free – can be ineffective without brand awareness
Free Job Boards	Free – considered ineffective for finding sales agents
Social Media	Free or paid - depending on the type and value
Paid Online Ads	$99 - $995/per geographic location
Searchable Databases	From $99/month to thousands of dollars
Online Trade Sites	$250 or more (more traffic means higher cost)
Business Publications	$500 or more depending on readership
Major Daily Newspaper	$2,000 plus (the ad often only runs 2-3 days)
Trade Shows	Cost of attendance or a display booth
Recruiting Company	10-20% of first year compensation program
Sales Agent Search Firms	Fees depend on search program requirements

Referrals – Asking for referrals is the best and often the simplest way of connecting with potential sales agents. Unfortunately most people will not spend the time and effort needed to build their referral network. To capitalize on referrals you need to contact companies that currently sell your products or your competitors' products and simply ask them whom they buy from. You will be surprised to find that most companies will share this information with you. Once you have a few names and their contact information the next step is to make the phone call to determine if they are open to discussing new opportunities. The goal of your first phone call is not to sign them up; it's simply to determine if they are open to discussing your opportunity.

Career Page on Your Website – This is a simple process. You create a landing page and advertise for sales agents. This process may not be successful unless you have a good flow of traffic to your website or unless your public relations and advertising programs are generating interest. This is a very inexpensive search method but if this is your only recruiting method, don't expect a fast response. Most small to mid-sized companies that I interviewed report they haven't had any success with a sales agent career page on their website.

Free Job Boards – The benefit of free job boards is they don't cost you anything to use but historically they have not been very successful for most companies. You can spend a lot of time advertising only to receive junk mail responses. If you are going to use free job boards I would recommend you create a "disposable" email account that you can shut it down if you are only getting junk mail responses. Beware - a lot of people who apply for sales agent's positions on the free job boards are really looking for full time paid work. They will quit the commission only job as soon as they find what they really want.

Social Media – There is a tremendous amount of buzz today around the use of social media for recruiting all types of business people, however many organizations that currently use this method to search for qualified sales agents are reporting less than satisfactory results. Unfortunately the hype is created by the social media industry itself and in many cases is seriously overblown. You can use paid social media recruiting and free social media recruiting but before you commit your budget to this you should have a clear understanding of your target market and the expected results.

Paid Online Ads – This method can produce results if you have targeted your paid ads in the places where your potential sales agents will see them. The more focused the niche, the more expensive the ads, the greater the potential for success. By the same token, if your industry has not historically used agents then you could be spending money on a lost cause.

Searchable Databases - A couple of good examples of this type of service are the US based www.RepHunter.net, and www.MANAonline.org. They have created databases containing thousands of pre-qualified sales agents. They can be searched for free based on the market, industry, territory or other keywords. You will have to pay for the opportunity to view the agents contact information once you review their profile. I have listed more resources at the back of this book.

Online Trade Publications –This option is very similar to business publications. Ask for information on the profile of their audience and the costs before you purchase any advertising with them.

Business Print Publications – Posting ads in publications is expensive and will only be successful if a potential sales agent is a subscriber. Before you commit to this type of advertising make sure you request a full disclosure of the publication's target audience so you can determine if there are sales agents in their database.

Major Daily Newspapers – Purchasing an ad in a newspaper is very expensive and most ads only run for a 2 or 3 days. Their ability to attract sales agents may not be cost justified. I can't report that anyone has ever told me they were successful using a newspaper ad.

Trade Shows – This is one of the best places to look for potential sales agents. The best method is to post a sign on your booth "Sales Agent Opportunities." This will invite any sales agents to meet with you and discuss the opportunity. Make sure you have a detailed fact find when you talk to the agents so you don't waste your time. The second trade show method is to simply attend the show and try to network with vendors and agents who may be attending. This method may not work as well and can cause animosity if you are just walking around the show searching for potential agents. Companies pay a lot of money to exhibit at a show and are not usually very receptive to people who are only hunting for agents at their booth.

Recruiting Companies – A very small number of recruiting firms have experience with sales agents and will undertake recruiting programs in this field. Be cautious if this is not an area of specialization and check for references to ensure they have a successful history of finding sales agents. Costs for this type of service will vary depending on the firm but expect to pay high search fees.

Sales Agent Search Firms - If you conduct a Google™ search for recruiting firms or placement agencies that focus on sales agents you will be hard pressed to find more than a handful in this niche. A few firms like B2B Sales Connections do exist but most are in very specialized markets or industries. The cost of hiring a sales agent search firm may run from a few thousand dollars to tens of thousands of dollars depending on the program but you will save a lot of time and aggravation and can expect to be connected with qualified sales agents very quickly. Look for a good track record and a guarantee of results before you hire a search firm.

Other Places to Search

- Government Directories
- Yellow Pages™ – online version will give quick access
- Industry Specific Seminars – network with peers and ask about agents
- Competitive Websites – they often list their business partners
- LinkedIn Groups – just about every industry has a members group
- Industry Experts – give them a call and ask for advice or referrals
- Create your own road show and invite local sales agents to attend

The Sales Agent Recruiting Process

Identifying potential sales agents is often the most difficult and time consuming part of the recruiting process. In the previous sections we identified our potential customers and their specific marketplace and now it's time to find key agents who can begin the process of increasing your market share.

The investment you make in your recruiting program will directly determine how quickly you can be selling your product through a sales agent channel. If you have a very small budget for recruiting then you can expect a longer time frame between the time you start recruiting and when you will start seeing sales results. If you create an aggressive recruiting program then you can expect to be making sales sooner.

Using job boards, ads, social media and other passive recruiting methods can require months of searching to find qualified business partners. This method will be very low cost but labour and time intensive. The other option is to target specific industries, markets, prospects and actively recruit them for your network. This method will cost more in the short term but should result in a channel that is producing revenue much faster.

Many companies believe the best method to identify prospective sales agents is to research them based on SIC codes, NAICS codes, territory or other key search terms. While this type of search may work in some industries a better method of developing prospecting lists is to look for your prospects' affinities or niches, such as trade associations, memberships in marketplace specific organizations, buying groups or other targeted processes. Consider the rifle versus the shotgun approach to recruiting. The more precise you can be with your identification process, the better your chance of finding qualified agents.

The problem with the SIC and NAICS codes is that often the small agents are listed under broad headings which are not very helpful or they're not listed at all. You may also end up purchasing an expensive list that is filled with companies but only a few are focused on the industry segment you are looking to approach.

In the Additional Resources section at the back of the book I have listed associations and websites that you can use as a starting point for your search. Often there are trade associations which will list their members for free on a website or in a publication. If a list is not available free of charge you could try and join the group as a vendor and get access to the membership lists that way. This type of listing or directory is controlled by the association and they make their money by selling advertising in their magazine, on their website and through other methods. Sometimes the only way to get a complete list is to have someone manually go through the directory and copy all the members' names into a CRM program or spreadsheet which you can use for prospecting. It may be time consuming but it should be inexpensive and the payoff will be a better recruiting process.

Remember, a sales agent is looking for what they perceive to be a compelling business opportunity. *Focus on the benefits you can offer them and what it means to their business:* increased income, attractive commissions and growth opportunities for new products.

Contacting Potential Sales Agents

Before we continue to the stage where you actually begin to contact agents let me once again reiterate the importance of being fully prepared. If you do not have an information package prepared in advance and an outline of your action plan then you are not ready to start contacting potential agents. If, on the other hand, you have completed the preliminary work, then you should be ready to go.

Consider your sales agent search as a dating process. You start with catching their attention and moving on to meeting for coffee. If that goes well then you schedule a dinner and if you are both still interested, you may begin to think about a long term relationship. If you are familiar with the marketing acronym *AIDA* (C.P Russell, 1921) you can apply this model to the process of generating interest from potential agents. AIDA stands for Attention, Interest, Desire, and Action.

Your first communication with the agent is all about getting their attention and creating the chemistry. A lot of people contend your initial contact with a potential sales agent should never be by email. I disagree with this statement because I have used email successfully hundreds of times over the years as a way to open the door. When I have identified a potential agent it's a quick method of giving them an overview of the opportunity to let them determine if it is interesting. I always follow up with a phone call in 3-4 business days if I don't hear back from them.

I find that many of prospects I contact by email are very quick to respond. In some cases it's a polite 'no thank you, I don't have the time' or 'it's not in my target market' but in most cases they are agreeable to a phone conversation to discuss the opportunity further.

If you don't have their direct email address then by all means a phone call or targeted letter may be your only solution for the first contact. Whatever methods you choose to employ for your first contact just remember you are not selling your product, you are looking for chemistry to open the door for a discussion about an opportunity.

The message must capture their attention and then generate interest in finding out more about your business. This is not the time to release the floodgates of information on your company and your products. You are only looking to make a connection and to start a conversation.

Use a 1-2 punch. Your first message should be short, direct and targeted, offering respondents a more comprehensive information package. Offering the prospective agent an exclusive new product opportunity can be a great call to action. As an example you could start your copy with "*Unique sales agent opportunity in Toronto with proven revenue stream.*" The second step should be a more comprehensive outline of the opportunity.

If you don't want to make your first contact by email them by all means pick up the phone and call them directly. My philosophy is use whatever method works best for you. The big take away is to take action and make the call or send the email. Whatever method you choose just be sure you are persistent. People are busy and very few will be interested in your opportunity. In fact a good agent who is in demand will most likely be too busy to take the time to speak with you. You may have to call or email them many times before you finally make contact.

Jeff Simon, CEO of the website *RepHunter, Inc.,* highlights the importance of follow-up with potential agents. His advice to people who are searching for sales agents is to remember that "placing productive reps is a 'numbers' game. If you make one or two attempts to contact an agent and then quit because you have not heard back from them then you are not going to be successful." As the old saying goes *'those who give up, lose. Those who persist, win.''* The secret is persistence. When you finally get the person on the phone you'd better have a great presentation to capture their interest.

If your product is viewed by potential agents as just another commodity your efforts to engage them will not be successful. If you are not getting any bites then consider reworking your approach. Or, if agents are engage at first then tune out as you precede, find out what's missing in your proposal and why they've lost interest. If you have the confidence to call the agent back when they dismiss your product you may be able to find out what's holding them back. It may not be something you can change for that agent but it can help you refine your message before you approach other potential agents.

You must also consider how many agents you are looking to work with in your alternate sales channel plan. Can you afford the time and resources to work with a single agent or are you looking to establish a team of agents across the country. In my experience you will often need to connect with 20 or more "qualified" sales agents before you find 1 that is interested in your product or service. I regularly tell companies that they should expect to invest anywhere from 20 to 40 hours over 30 to 60 days in the search process to find 1 qualified agent. In some cases where the product was viewed by potential agents as just another commodity the company was not success at all.

In the interest of full disclosure B2B Sales Connections Inc. is a paid subscriber to *RepHunter* and we have not received any compensation for this endorsement. We have been using *RepHunter* for years to help our clients identify potential sales agents. It is simple to search, inexpensive to use and provides a good description of the agents. However, you still must be ready to work hard at connecting with any agents that you identify as potential business partners. It may not be right for your industry but since the initial search is free it is always worthwhile to try.

> ⚠ Anti- Spam laws require unsolicited commercial e-mail messages to be labeled (though not by a standard method) and to include opt-out instructions and the sender's physical address. It is important that you check your local and national regulations before you send email to a company or individual that has not given you their contact information.

Pierre Carriere has spent over 30 years in the rep business. He is currently the president of BEXSA Solutions Inc. a corporation focused on developing sales into the market for embedded solutions addressing industrial, medical, military and OEM customers. Here are his thoughts on the recruiting of sales agents.

What are the best practices you see from the companies that do it right?
Pierre; "*They generate leads for us and are outstanding in their support. If I have a problem and need an answer, I can't' afford to wait a few days before someone gets back to me. The smart partners provide answers in 24 hours or less. I am also looking for a strong relationship with the companies channel manager.*"

When a potential new business partner approaches you, what are you looking for?
Pierre; "*They must complement my current line of products. They should have products that my customers are asking for. I want to know they are committed to the use of a sales agent channel and not just 'testing the waters'. I need to know if they are generating leads and have existing sales. Finally, if they are expecting us to do pioneering work, I am going to consider a retainer for all the ground work we will have to do at our expense.*"

What are some of the major changes you have seen recently in your business?
Pierre; "*I have steadily watched companies try to drive our commission down even though we are the ones that get their products in the door in the first place.*"

What are the pain points when dealing with manufacturers or principals?
Pierre; "*It's a growing problem trying to work with companies that don't pay on time. The contract dictates the terms so abide by them. A number of companies have been guilty of setting up multiple reps but not clearly defining the territory or market. In some cases they just don't care. We don't find out about the other agent until we both start competing in the same account with the same product. It really doesn't help the relationship. House accounts are another problem we have to deal with.*"

What's your view on the future of Independent Sales Agents?
Pierre; "*As more companies are looking for cost savings you are going to see a move towards more sales outsourcing. The agent business is poised for growth. Agents are going to play a very important role as more international companies are trying to break into the North American market. It's very difficult, expensive and not very effective to send people over from other countries and expect them to survive in a completely new market.*"

www.bexsasolutions.com

You Need a Clear and Compelling Message

Before you approach a potential sales agent by phone you must be able to clearly and concisely communicate your unique value proposition. You have to grab the agent's attention in less than 15 seconds and deliver a message within the first minute that will open up a dialogue. If your company is not known to the prospect then the chances of getting 10 or 15 minutes to ramble on about your great products are very slim. Remember the KISS rule – Keep it short and simple.

Secondly, the message must target your unique value proposition from the agent's point of view. You must quickly explain how it will help them accomplish their goals and improve their business. Your message must focus on the agent, not "what your product does for the customer." Your message must grab the interest of the sales agent in terms of how it will help them grow their business first then how it will impact their customers second.

Here's an example:

A client manufactures and sells hand sanitizer products. Their primary target customers are hospitals, long-term care facilities and seniors' residents. They were looking to set up a sales channel using agents that currently call on this vertical market.

Their Approach - Originally the company was calling prospective sales agents and would start the conversation explaining that they were a leading manufacturer of hand sanitizers and cleaning products and were looking for a sales agent. The level of interest they received from sales agents was zero. Most agents saw the product as a commodity and their customers always bought the lowest price.

Our Solution – We redesigned the initial communication for the company. Instead of leading with hand sanitizer (price sensitive commodity) we approached the potential agents with a different message. We learned that if a hospital wing or patient care facility was shut down because of the threat of infections it was a major crisis that was costly and could ruin the health care facility's reputation. Instead of leading with "hand sanitizers" sales agents were approached with a different message: *"Would you be interested in learning about a product that prevents the outbreak of infection which could potentially shut down your customer's facility?"*

This time they had the prospective sales agent's attention. The company then went on to discuss the opportunity and how it could help the sales agent grow their business by educating its customers about infection control. They were still selling hand sanitizers and cleaning products but "infection control" was the value added magic phrase that generated the interest. Cleaning product or hand sanitizer was not the message that interested the sales agents.

To make a pitch like this work effectively, you must have a clearly defined message before you approach a prospective sales agent. Once you have the message you need to revise the information as you start the recruiting process and determine what specific benefits you bring to the relationship.

Let me include a quick note about pre-call research. Very often we, as salespeople, spend more time researching the prospect's background instead of just "identifiying" the prospect problems and then initiating the first contact. As author and sales trainer Susan Enns says: "we don't wait for all the traffic lights to turn green before we pull out of the driveway and the same rule should apply to prospecting. Don't try to get it perfect, just get it done."

When I search for sales agents for customers I have a few key criteria that I use to determine who I will contact. It's often more productive than trying to spend hours researching an agent before I make first contact. With agents you usually can't find much information about them anyway. Most don't have a website and are not listed on Dun and Bradstreet, Hoovers, even LinkedIn. My recommendation – pick up the phone and make the call.

One further point to consider. If the agent is not intersted, always, always, always ask them if they know of any other agents that may be better suited for your product. Remember the sales tip: "if you don't ask, the answer is always no."

Coaching Exercise 7 – Phone Template: First Contact

Sample Script –

Hi Tom, this is Fred Ford calling from Riff Raff Manufacturing. I understand you are a sales agent that calls on hospitals and long term care facilities. Fred, would you be interested in learning about a new product that could prevent the outbreak of infections that could potentially shut down your customers' facilities?

Tom: Yes I would, tell me more.

Fred*: Well Tom, this is a great opportunity for sales agents who currently sell _____ and call on _____. In fact we already have successful agents that call on similar accounts. Can I ask you a few questions about your business to determine if this opportunity may be a fit for both of us?*

Tom: Yes.

If the agent is open to the discussion this would be a good time to go to the sales agent fact find document you have created and begin to learn more about their business.

Follow-up questions:

1) Who do you primarily call on?

    a. _____

    b. _____

    c. _____

2) What are the main product lines you sell?

    a. _____

    b. _____

    c. _____

    d. _____

3) Are you an independent sales agent or part of a multi-rep group?

    a. Single agent

    b. Multi-rep agency

4) What territory is your primary area of focus? _____

5) Are you looking for new lines that can complement your current product offering if they can provide a good return on your time invested (ROTI)?

    a. Yes _____   No_____   Too early to judge _____

Coaching Exercise 8 – Email Template: First Contact

Below is an example of an email template used to make first contact with sales agents. The email is very short, contains lots of key words and white space to make it easy to scan and read. This standard format has been successful for many of our clients with only minor variations depending on the company's products or services. In this case, by using a keyword search, we already know that the potential sales agents call on the type of customers listed in the email.

Sample Email Template –

Subject – Sales Agent Opportunity – Merchandising Displays

Dear _____:

I understand that your current customer list focuses on the following?

- Retail stores that use display cases
- Jewellery, watch and sunglass manufacturers

The difference between a cheap, poorly made display unit and a quality display cabinet will affect your retail customer's bottom line.

Our current sales agents report the time between qualifying the prospect and closing the sale is less than 30 days and pays over $3,000 in commission. As a manufacturer of custom displays we can help you serve your customers better and increase the value of each order. We can provide a uniquely designed, attractive, and price competitive display system for your customers and you win with a new revenue stream.

If you are serious about expanding your product line, and providing new services to your existing customers and opening new doors then you are invited to learn more about this opportunity.

This product will provide an excellent opportunity for a motivated sales agent.

- Excellent commissions
- Growing market
- Select territories and markets available

For more information about this opportunity and our products please reply to this email and I will arrange a phone meeting within the next 48 hours.

Regards,

Name
Position
Phone Contact
Email Contact
Website –
Unsubscribe info – to comply with C-Spam rules

Included 2 brief testimonials

Attracting Sales Agents to Your Website

If building an alternate sales channel using sales agents is part of the long term growth strategy for your company then you should consider dedicating a portion of your website to the recruiting process. This can be accomplished in a number of ways.

By creating a new heading on your website which promotes opportunities to become a business partner you are opening the door for independent sales agents and resellers to find out more about the program and at the same time capturing their information for follow-up. Inviting potential sales agents to contact you directly will help to develop a stream of "prequalified" candidates. It is always easier to work with a warm lead that came looking for your product than to dial a cold call that may not connect with the prospect at the right time.

When designing the landing page for your potential business partner describe the opportunity, but briefly, without giving too much information. You want to focus on WIIFT (what's in it for them). The goal is to get prequalified leads from potential partners. Once you have this information you want to quickly contact the prospect to begin the discussion process. You must have a service commitment that assures the prospect that you will respond to their inquiry within 24 hours. This is going to be your first contact with the potential partner and you must start the "dating" process on the right foot by letting them experience what it is like for them to do business with you. If you take days or weeks to respond to a "hot lead" from a prospective sales agent then you are sending the wrong message to them.

KISS – Using the KISS principal, keep the amount of information you provide about the opportunity short and simple and when you request their contact information just ask for the bare minimum. There is no need at this time to collect anything more than the contact's name, company name, email, phone number and their website address. This will give you enough information to contact the prospect and quickly investigate their business. The idea is to open the lines of communication so they begin to connect with you, this is not a pre-screening process so do not request too much information at this point in time.

Business Partner Program

Opportunity – From time to time Widgets Are Us has openings for sales agents and sales professionals in specific territories

Qualifications – If you have a technical background in Widget sales or are a qualified widget product developer we would like to hear from you to discuss the opportunity to join our growing team

Apply Now – Simply click on the Apply Now link below and submit your information. A member of our business development team will respond to you within 1 business day.

Whenever possible, it is best to have a specific link on your website that allows a person to apply directly to you. If you don't have the technical ability to create a separate link then you can create an email message box that opens with a specific address dedicated to the agent program. The problem with an email box is you can't control the information the prospect provides so you may receive a lot of irrelevant information or spam, whereas with the controlled link you force the prospect to include specific data in order to activate the submit function.

The goal of the website landing page is simply to attract prequalified sales agents, direct sales people and resellers to your company. However, this should never be your only method of recruiting business partners. A program of this nature is very passive and may attract a limited number of prospects especially in the early stages. If immediate growth is a concern then you need a more aggressive search process.

I am not going to elaborate on search engine optimization to generate more traffic to your website. If you are not getting leads for your products or services then this is an area where you need to improve. According to current studies almost 90% of buyers are starting their research online and have a good understanding of the products or services they want long before they contact your company looking for information or pricing. If your website is not generating leads then you need to seriously look at updating the content and possibly its functionality. With more and more people now accessing websites from their tablets or mobile devices it is critical that you use a format that is compatible with these products and not just computer display screens.

Content: To attract agents you need to consider adding educational content as a method of engaging them. If someone is first drawn to your content and sees you as an authority in your industry then they are more likely to be interested in your business process. Think educational material not marketing brochures!

Testimonials: If you already have a number of sales agents who are successful then add testimonials or case studies to your website. If a potential agent can read how your current business partners have succeeded they will be more inclined to want to get involved.

Sales Ready Messages: In the reference section at the back of the book we have created a number of sales ready messages as examples for some of the documentation you will need. These include telemarketing scripts and email templates. You should create your own scripts and templates as you build your *Sales Agent Playbook.*

Outsourced Sales Agent Search Programs

Using an outsourced search company is often the fastest and most cost effective way to identify and contact prospective agents. While there are tens of thousands of companies that offer recruiting services to help employers find direct sales people, there are only a handful of companies that specialize in finding sales agents and manufacturer's representatives.

While online sales agent search sites are considered much like dating services, meaning they will connect you with potential sales agents but the rest is up to you, outsourced sales agent search programs will play the match maker role and help you take the courtship further.

In order to help you find sales agents these company, for a fee, will search for potential sales agents, make the initial and follow up contacts, pre-screen, interview, provide reference checks and some will even help you with the design and implement your entire recruiting and on-boarding process.

A B2B sales agent search company (http://www.b2bsalesconnections.com/agents.php) can quickly contact a large number of previously identified prospects, determine their interest and ability to take on new products, and report back with a short list for follow-up. In just a few days they can contact a list of prospects that would take you weeks to call and pre-screen. If you are looking to move quickly and lack experienced personnel to do this type of work then you should consider outsourcing all or a portion of your recruiting program to a professional services sales agent search firm.

If you choose to use a sales agent search company make sure you conduct your own due diligence on both the search company and the sales agents they recommend. The final decision on who to hire will always be yours.

Never get pressured into signing an agent that you are not convinced will be a good fit for your business. If the sales agent search firm gets paid a finder's fee when you hire one of their candidates be sure you have a guarantee that protects you if the agent doesn't work out in the first 3 to 6 months. Most placement firms will offer at least a 90 day replacement guarantee.

Designing a Sales Agent Information Package

Once you have contacted a potential sales agent you must be ready with your information package. This stage of the recruiting process will usually make or break the new relationship. All too often a manufacturer has successfully engaged a prospective sales agent only to have the recruiting process stall or evaporate because the company was not prepared for the next step. You must have a comprehensive overview of the opportunity, your product, and your company ready to share with the sales agent. If you try to 'wing it' here you will quickly lose their interest and be back to square one.

If you are looking for ideas for a sales agent information package look no further than the home pages for one of the thousands of franchise companies. You can even request a few different franchise marketing kits to get a good idea how they approach their potential partners. Sites like www.franchising.com and www.cfa.ca are good places to start. They list many franchise industries and chances are there is something close to your industry which can provide you with great insight on how to approach a potential partner. Always ask yourself when you are looking at another company's recruiting program: Are they answering the question 'what's in it for me,' or are they simply selling the features of their products?

According to Industry Canada almost 96% of small businesses (those from 1 to 99 employees) that enter the marketplace survive for one full year, 85% survive for three years and 70% last for 5 years (*Key Small Business Statistics - January 2009.*)

Furthermore, Statistics Canada, (*Failing Concerns: Business Bankruptcy in Canada*, 1997,) reports that most businesses fail because of weak general management, weak financial management, or weak marketing capabilities. Since 2000, the US has not kept statistics on the failure rates of businesses which have only one employee. The National Federation of Independent Businesses (NFIB) estimates that over the lifetime of a business 39% are profitable, 30% break even, and 30% lose money, with 1% falling in the "unable to determine" category. Any way you look at it the chance of success can be very slim for a small business but having a plan and employing the right resources can help you improve your chances.

Since the franchise model is built on the foundation of a documented repeatable system which can be taught to anyone, the failure rate of a franchise is usually very low if you follow the program. Many franchise operations are so strong that they are viewed as a license to print money.

If you take the time to create a documented repeatable program for your sales agents then you can expect a much higher success rate than if you just try and make it up as you go along and expect them to do the same.

There is an added benefit to having everything documented and repeatable. Companies which have defined repeatable processes in place are more valuable when the owner is considering selling the business. Many small to mid-sized businesses are only valuable as long as the owner is in control. Once they leave, the company implodes because the guiding force is gone. If you create a company that can operate without the owner's hands-on involvement then you have developed a viable business that will be more valuable when you go to sell it in the future. Take the time to build a proper structure.

> To grow, a company must either attract new customers or sell more to their existing customers. When designing a sales agent marketing kit be sure to incorporate how you can help them accomplish these goals by becoming your business partner.

Components of a Sales Agent Info Package

What information do you need in your agent information package? First of all remember you are not trying to sell the prospect on everything you do. The purpose is simply to get them interested in taking the next step in the process and to do this you need to include the following:

- Description of your solution - Supporting quantifiable documentation on how you save customers money or time, solve a problem, fill a need, or create a solution to grow their business.

- Company information (not the annual report version) – This needs to be crafted specifically to show your expertise in the industry, past successes and projected future growth. Talk about opportunities and accomplishments not history.

- Description of the opportunity – List existing business, potential business and marketplace research.

- Product information – If you have "raving fans" and great testimonials, this is the place to load them up. Agents are looking for products that "sell themselves" and the better your brand awareness and acceptance the easier your channel development.

- Call to action with deadline – You have 5 days to contact us to express your interest before we approach one of your competitors as our sole representative in your territory.

Other information you will need:

- Marketing and advertising plans, product or service literature
- Sales agent commission structure or compensation program
- Organizational overview and references
- Sales agent agreement (contract)
- Price book

The Sales Agent Agreement

Now that you have identified your potential business partners you will need to have a signed Sales Agent Agreement or Sales Agent Contract in place before you move forward. We have created an agreement checklist to ensure you have covered most of the information which is commonly required in this type of document. By reviewing the checklist you should be able to determine what information will be needed in your own document. If you would like a copy of a sample sales agent agreement template please visit our website at http://www.b2bsalesconnections.com/store.php and select *Sales Agent Recruiting Toolkit.*

Most lawyers do not draft this type of document on a regular basis so it can be expensive and time consuming for them to create a one-off contract for you. By approaching them with a framework for your sales agent agreement you are saving time, money and ensuring you do not forget to include important information. Your lawyer may suggest additional terms and conditions or remove portions from the sample but at least it gives them a framework for the document. The last thing you want to do is attract great potential agents and then have them bail out of the negotiations at the last minute because of concerns about your complicated contract.

I have seen independent sales agent agreements which were 6 or 7 pages in length and others that ran over 300 pages. Guess which ones scared off the potential agent? If the sales agent needs to hire a lawyer to understand all the terms and conditions in the document then chances are they won't sign it. The more complicated the agreement the more likely it focuses on every possible contingency for protecting the company that wrote the agreement rather than the agent signing it. Massive agreements are also a signal to the agent that here have been serious problems in the past which lead to each and every clause being added. If the company has experienced that much trouble with their sales channel in the past is an agent really going to want to work with them?

When recruiting business partners the one suggestion we have is to keep the legal agreement short and simple. Protect your company and be fair to your potential partners. If your agents see a complicated 100 page contract they may be concerned you have something to hide.

If you keep it simple and easy to understand with logical terms and conditions it will make the partnership start off on the right foot. We strongly suggest you consult with an attorney before entering into any agreements

Another way to proceed is to first create a sales agent letter of intent. This type of document is often used prior to signing a full scale agreement. It can be used to establish the ground rules for a potential agent so they can begin to represent your products while you evaluate their commitment to the program. A sample letter of intent is included in the reference section at the back of the book.

Sales Agent On-Boarding Checklist

When a company is selling a franchise business to a new prospect they have all the necessary documentation developed well in advance of the process. Once the franchise agreement is signed, the complete training program documentation is delivered to the new owner immediately. This will include: sales and product training programs, schedules and specifics on every aspect of the business process. As a company working with sales agents, it is critical that you also have all your sales, service, marketing, training, administrative and any other required material completed before you sign your first contract. What happens in the first few days after the contract is signed will affect how your business partners see your company in the future.

Do you remember starting a new sales job? The first day you showed up excited to be part of a new organization? Likely it went like this: You met the new boss and were shown to your work area and put right to work. Often times the only training and support you received from the company was "here's your desk, your phone and your business cards; now get out and sell."

This type of introduction is discouraging to a new employee. The people who hired you may have spent weeks or months determining if you were the right person to join their organization and then spent time convincing you they were the right company, and then they dropped the ball once you started. You walked through the door that first day and discovered it was all an illusion. You're hired, now get to work. No official welcome, no time spent introducing you to the people you will be working with, no tour of the facilities, and certainly no attempt to make you feel as if you were part of a team.

How we introduce new employees into a company and how we welcome a new sales agent to your program will determine the long term survival of our organizations. People want to belong but we must provide meaningful engagement and allow them to develop and grow.

Regardless of whether it is a new employee in your administration, a manager, shipper, sales person or accounting clerk, by creating a 90 day success plan you will set the stage for their tenure at your organization. When everyone knows what's expected of them and how their role fits into the operation of the organization you will create a successful corporate culture.

Why do people line up to join IBM, Microsoft, Xerox, Toyota, Apple and Google? It happens because they invest in and promote human capital. They celebrate training and professional development and they challenge people to be innovative. There's a huge benefit if you engage agents. For companies that do it right, their sales agent team turnover is lower. People won't want to leave if they feel appreciated, and the result will be happier customers and a more successful company.

You need to have the same process in place before you recruit your first sales agent. On the following page there is a sample Sales Agent On-boarding Checklist that you can modify to create one for your sales agents or sales staff.

Sales Agent On-Boarding Plan Checklist

Sales Agent: _____

Program Start Date: _____

	Completed
Completed Documentation	
• Sales Agent Agreement Signed and Filed	☐
• Sales Agent Agreement Copies Returned	☐
• 90 Day Success Plan for Sales Agent Discussed	☐
Company Procedures and Order Processing Training	
• Company Procedures Discussion	☐
• Sales Order Paperwork Process	☐
• Sample Orders	☐
• Creation of Briefcase Paperwork File	☐
• Order Processing Training Included in Sales Training Schedule	☐
• Payment Terms – Order timelines – other financial issues	☐
Sales Agent Compensation Program	
• Compensation Plan Discussion	☐
• Territory Assignment Discussion	☐
• Compensation Plan Acknowledgement Form	☐
• Price Books and e-Documents distributed	☐
• Annual Sales Targets – Discussed and sign off	☐
Product Training	
• Product Knowledge Training Schedule Worksheet	☐
• Training on the Competition	☐
Sales Training	
• Sales Training Schedule Worksheet	☐
• Follow-up File or CRM System Creation	☐
Service and Technical Support	
• Warranties, Guarantees	☐
• Parts and replacements	☐
• Who to contact for what and when	☐
Performance Expectation and Monitoring	
• Shared Expectations Discussion	☐
• Sales Reporting, Activity Tracking and Forecasting	☐

This checklist is intended to be an aid in creating your own on-boarding process checklist for your sales agent program.

Immediate Actions Items

Have you completed all of the following?

- ☐ Training program information – Training manuals
- ☐ Training schedule 30 to 90 days
- ☐ Appointed a channel manager
- ☐ Determined administrative support person(s)
- ☐ Assigned service support or technical support staff
- ☐ Addressed your internal corporate concerns
- ☐ Potential revenue for territory – and sales goal for agent
- ☐ Competition and competitive activity guide
- ☐ Channel conflict guidelines
- ☐ Outlined how to address competition between sales agents if they overlap
- ☐ Outline how to address conflict between agents and direct sales reps if it occurs
- ☐ Published a price book

Legal advice obtained for –

- ☐ Non-disclosure document, non-compete and non-solicitation agreement
- ☐ Sales agent agreement
- ☐ Termination notices, non-performance clauses and warning letters

Published a policy for –

- ☐ Return of products
- ☐ Payment terms - Commission payments to agents
- ☐ Reversal of commission if end user fails to pay
- ☐ Price changes
- ☐ Warranties and guarantees
- ☐ Service costs to sales agents
- ☐ Trademarks, trade names, registered product names
- ☐ Conflict between sales channels

Three most important concepts I learned in this chapter:

1) _____

2) _____

3) _____

Chapter 5 – Managing Your Alternate Channel

In this chapter we are going to move into the foundation of the program and the management of your sales agents. If you follow the articles and blogs that are prevalent in social media you will find that communication or lack thereof is a frequent topic and one of the biggest concerns from both agents

> *Communication is the foundation for your sales channels success*

and principals. In sales we regularly debate the fine line between good follow up and becoming annoying to the person with whom you are trying to communicate.

When you are working with your agents you need to be timely with your communication and follow up if you want to be successful. If you aren't communicating with them on a weekly basis then you are going to lose their interest and focus. Subsequently, if you lose their focus they will stop selling your product and maybe even start selling a competitor's product if they are more effective at engaging them.

As the national sales channel manager for a technology company we were able to grow our business by over 39% annually over a 5 year period. We didn't have a radical new product, or cutting edge technology and we were by far the highest priced product in the market. What we did was train and communicate with our agent partners on a weekly basis and sometimes daily if necessary. We solved their problems quickly, we gave them accurate answers and we supported them as rock star sales people whenever possible. As a result our agents focused on our products because we made it as easy for them to be successful. With the support they received from our team they had no need to look for new products or focus on other manufacturers. We worked constantly on the relationship and they rewarded us with exponential sales growth.

Your goal should be to create an exceptional support team for your sales agents. To do this you need clear lines of communication, great training and constant support. Not only should you be providing feedback to the agents, they should also be sending information back to you based on their industry knowledge and relationships with the customers.

One of the most important steps you can take to build your channel is to have a dedicated person in your company who is responsible for the growth and well-being of the channel. Not only will this person be a liaison between your company and the sales agents, he or she will also be responsible for representing the interests of the agents back to the company executives.

If you are a small organization then this can be accomplished by an administrative support person, provided they have the backing and support of the key executives. If you are a larger company you should consider a dedicated channel sales manager. If you are planning to build a team of 8 to 10 agents or more then you will absolutely need a channel sales manager responsible for the programs operation.

The Channel Sales Manager – A Key Component

The skills required to become a successful channel sales manager are very different from the skills needed to manage a direct sales force. As a manager in charge of a direct sales force you are in constant contact with your sales people and you should be able to frequently work with them in the field. Since a direct sales person is employed by your company you have control over most of their business activities. The same does not hold true when you are working with a group of independent sales agents.

The role of the channel sales manager is very different from that of a sales manager of a direct sales team. First and foremost, the sales agents are for all legal purposes independent business people. You don't have the same control over their activities and the relationship is usually at arm's length. You have to focus more on influence than on control.

Channel managers often spend most of their time working with their sales agents in an effort to keep them focused on selling their products since they will have access to many different suppliers. Don't forget, they will also represent other manufacturers and suppliers that are constantly vying for their loyalty. We have always found the secret to success when working with independent sales agents is to constantly work to strengthen the relationship you have developed and improve the opportunities that you provide.

As a Channel Sales Manager You Are:

- A liaison between your sales agents and your company
- A coach, mentor and trainer to help your agents grow and succeed
- Support for your channel partners in difficult sales situations
- An expert on your products or services
- A resource for your agents
- A trusted advisor to your channel partners
- Required to monitor your partners' performance and provide feedback
- Representing the interests of your company
- Striving to improve sales in your channel
- Looking to create a win-win-win situation

As a Channel Sales Manager You Are Not:

- A direct sales person – don't sell for them, teach them how to sell
- The administration department – you need to focus on selling time
- The service department –put them in touch with the right people
- A free consultant – focus on what makes you and your agents money

Show How – Don't Do For!

One of our clients had a channel sales manager who by all accounts was doing an excellent job. The sales agents respected the work the manager did for them and were very impressed with the amount of business he was able to develop and close. The trouble was his travel expenses were out of control. The cost of each sale far exceeded the profit the company was making on the transaction. The payout to the sales agents was a fixed percentage of the selling price resulting in a good income for the agents but the manufacturer was losing money. The company was prepared to let the channel sales manager continue in hopes that he would grow the business to a profitable level in the coming year.

Upon investigating the channel manager's sales process further it turned out the agents were not actually doing any of the selling. The channel manager would frequently spend 3 or 4 days per month at the agents' locations. He would meet with customers, make the presentations, close the sale and then turn the paperwork in at the end of each day to the sales agent who would in turn submit the order. Of course the agents loved the channel manager. He did all the work. It cost them nothing and they were paid the full margin on every sale the channel manager made for them.

It quickly became clear that the channel sales manager was only successful when he was directly interacting with the customer. He was a good salesman but he did not have the necessary skills to teach the sales agents how to be successful. He could go out with an agent and close business but the agents could not generate their own business when he was not travelling with them.

Both he and the agents knew that it was a waste of time for him to make sales calls with the agent he was supposed to be training when he almost always closed the sale personally. Over time the agents just stopped going to appointments with him since they were still getting the full benefit of the sale without doing any work. Instead of teaching the sales agents how to sell the product and provide them with the necessary support he was doing all the work and the agents were making all the profit.

The manufacturer realized they needed to make a major change to the alternate channel program which meant rebuilding with a new channel manager who had the skills needed to train the sales agents to work independently. The sales agents did not like the new sales process and revolted, threatening to cancel their agreements and look for new products. The manufacturer on the other hand, refused to be threatened and accepted the sales agents' resignations and began to recruit new channel partners who would actively commit to selling their products.

Once a few agreements were cancelled and the new agent recruiting process started, a change of mind occurred. The sales agents realized the manufacturer was serious about instituting a new process and the channel partners knew they could not afford to have a competitor in their territory representing a product which was in high demand. As a result most of the original agents signed their agreements and took an active role in becoming true channel partners.

The real turnaround came over the next 6 months when the newly appointed channel manager instituted a formal sales agent training program and the monthly sales started to climb to levels that had never been seen before. Once all the agents knew what to do and how to do it their monthly results far exceeded what they could have done waiting for the channel manager to visit their territory and sell for them. The growth in the channel was exponential and sales agents who had been just getting by became selling machines with incredible results.

The manufacturer benefited as well because their cost of sale dropped significantly, the profit margin grew, and overall the volume of sales increased. The agents increased their business exponentially by learning how to attract more prospects, sell to more customers and increase the value of their customer base by increasing the average sale size as well as increasing the mix of products their customers purchased.

The lesson to be learned by this example is that your channel manager must be a teacher and coach to your sales agents, not a replacement sales person. A sales manager whose only job is to sell for weak or inexperienced sales people will have a very short life span. They will either burn out or spend all their time trying to figure out how to make more calls for ineffective sales people.

As an Alternate Channel Sales Manager your territory can be a group of sales agents in a small geographic area or it may encompass one country or even a group of countries. The product you sell and the number of agents on your team will determine how much area you can cover. From a corporate perspective the size of each territory will depend on the number of agents, the amount of support required and the time you need to spend with individual sales agents.

When setting up a new alternate sales channel it is important to prevent yourself from being spread too thin. If you recruit too many agents too quickly, the channel manager will not have time to train them or give them the support they need in the early stages of the relationship. Good agents will not hang around for long if you are not fully prepared to launch your program.

Promoting Your Top Gun to Channel Sales Manager

Many companies continue to make a critical error when they are looking internally to promote someone to the role of channel sales manager. All too often they take their best sales person and try to turn them into their channel sales manager with disastrous results. Your best sales person is no longer selling, profits drop, their current territory loses coverage, good customers may become disillusioned and defect and ultimately the sales person becomes frustrated with their failure in the new position.

Face it, they have not been trained in channel sales management and their confidence will plummet as the pressures to produce builds. Inevitably they decide to leave the organization and return to direct selling for either a competitor or another industry. This person almost never asks to return to their original sales role since it would mean admitting failure in front of the company and their peers.

If you are looking for a channel sales manager you should look beyond the top sales person and you will often find you have a good sales performer who is better suited to the management role. Once you have identified the individual you would like to promote to channel manager, you should conduct a thorough sales management assessment process. The cost of this service is very low and can be very helpful in determining if you have the proper candidate.

The next step is to provide sales management training from a company which is experienced in working with alternate sales management channels. A program of sales management training that focuses on direct selling techniques will not work for a manager who is going to be running a sales channel. They are very different.

Our advice is don't waste your money sending the new manager to an off the shelf "Sales Manager Training Course." If you want a training program that will make a difference, deliver results and provide a long term ROI then you need to look for a program which includes B2B knowledge based training (http://www.b2bsalesconnections.com/sales_training.php) that is focused on selling with independent sales agents in alternative sales channel envirnment. This will need to come from a company that is experienced in agent channel operations and management. This type of training is very different from the knowledge required to manage an in-house sales team.

To train your channel sales manager the provider must offer "one-on-one coaching" (http://www.b2bsalesconnections.com/coaching_services.php) to build competency through practice after the formal training is complete. Very few sales training companies offer this critical component. The best way for someone to learn a new skill and create lasting results is through the mentoring process. For your new channel sales manager to be successful you need a program that can provide this specialized alternate sales channel management support on the front end and ongoing coaching after the 'formal' part of the training is complete.

> *Studies show companies with a well-defined sales process consistently outperform those with no process. What message do you want to send to prospective sales agents?*

Your Sales Agent On-Boarding Process

The best Fortune 500 companies that leverage alternate sales channels have a structured "On-Boarding" process which every new independent sales agent must follow. The plan lays out detailed timelines and benchmarks, specific action items, and goals. This formal process is great for both the company and the new agent because it leaves nothing to interpretation and establishes accountabilities and shared expectations. The initial training is structured and detailed, giving your sales agent the knowledge and confidence that your organization has a plan and intends to help them succeed.

It is usually in small to mid-sized businesses that formal sales processes are neglected and problems occur bringing on new agents or new sales people. In most cases these are owner-operated companies where the on-boarding process and training falls to the owner or manager of a small sales team. Although the intentions are always good, potential sales agents report that the companies do not have a process in place and the agents spend valuable time trying to figure out what to do and how to do it. In addition, the new agent is often not sure what is expected of them in terms of direction and performance. "Welcome to the company. Here's your price book and brochures. Now go out and sell!" This not a recipe for success nor is it a viable on-boarding process.

By not having a process in place from the start the sales agent loses direction and becomes frustrated. The business owner is disappointed and fears they have made the wrong hiring decision. So how do you fix this problem? First, regardless of the size of your organization, you must develop a written plan which lays out specific actions, goals and timelines for the first 30, 60 and 90 days plus expectations for the first year. This may sound like a daunting task but it is actually much easier than you would think.

If you are the business owner and CoE (Chief of Everything) you should look for outside expertise (http://www.b2bsalesconnections.com/coaching_services.php) to assist you with this process. This will provide an inexpensive foundation for developing a quick start program that allows you to remain focused on activities which drive revenue. After all you most likely hired an accountant, web-designer, and IT firm so why would you attempt to self-manage the one area of your organization that will directly affect your top line. Each dollar in lost sales opportunities is revenue you will never recover.

The complete 90 day plan needs to include goals, activities, product training, competition, prospecting, order processing, customer service, market evaluations, performance metrics and simple things like helping the sales agent get to know your company and its people. Once you have a sales process in place your new agents will be highly motivated, more confident and better sales people.

As I mentioned in the first chapter, this is where most companies fall down. Just because you have found a sales agent who has industry experience does not mean you will develop a successful relationship. You will need a strong start to your on-boarding process and that means having an action plan or sales playbook ready to go.

Coaching Exercise 9 – The Sales Agent Playbook

To create your own **Action Plan for Sales Agent Success**™ you must be able to answer the following questions and have the answers clearly documented in your new agent sales playbook.

1) What problems do we solve?

2) Who are the best targets for this service/product?

3) How do we position ourselves in the marketplace?

    a. Who are our customers?

    b. What are their titles?

    c. How do we approach them?

4) What defines a good prospect for our business?

5) How do I generate leads?

6) What message should I be using to get an appointment with a prospect?

7) What questions should I be asking to pre-qualify prospects?

8) What are the steps in our sales process?

9) What objections should I expect?

    a. Price Objections

        i. How do we compare to our competitors?

        ii. How do we justify our pricing?

    b. Product Objections

        i. What can't we do?

        ii. What is unique about our product/service?

        iii. What are the main objections we hear?

    c. Competition

    d. Other _____

10) What information do I need to know to handle these objections?

11) Do you have sample scripts and templates for the following?

    a. Networking

    b. Phone call

    c. Email to new prospect

    d. Fact find questionnaire

    e. Proposal

    f. Objection handling

    g. Negotiation and closing

12) What is the reporting process?

    a. How will we communicate regularly?

    b. Do you hold regular sales meetings?

13) What goals will be set with the sales agent?

    a.   Total sales

    b.   New customer acquisition

    c.   Repeat business

14) How is the sales agent paid?

    a.   When

    b.   Process

    c.   Chargebacks, cancelled orders, non-payment

15) Organizational Structure - Who does the agent contact for information?

    a.   Technical matters

    b.   Shipping/Delivery

    c.   Installation

    d.   Accounting and administrative

    e.   Pricing

    f.   Sales/Marketing support

    g.   Other _____

Once completed, the *Sales Agent Playbook* should be distributed to your agents in two formats: an electronic version they can load onto their computer or tablet and refer to as they are learning about your products, your company and your procedures and a printed copy to keep handy for future reference.

You can also use the playbook as a recruiting tool. Nothing shows a potential sales agent you are focused and mean business like showing them a copy of the completed document. When they see the playbook, they know you already have a well thought out program.

The playbook makes their job much easier since they are not expected to make it up as they go along. With the playbook in place now all you have to do is schedule weekly or bi-weekly training seminars to familiarize them with your methods of finding, qualifying and closing prospects.

B2B Sales Connections **Action Based Sales Training Program** can be used to help you develop the right process for your alternate sales channel group and managers. Please visit our website www.b2bsalesconnections.com for more information.

Where Should You Conduct the Training Programs?

Since most sales agents work by themselves from a home office you will have to determine the best place for training. If the agent is located close to your offices then I would recommend that you conduct the training sessions on your premises. However, if the distance and cost of travel makes it difficult to conduct on-site training then you need to consider other options. While face-to-face meetings are always the best choice, properly designed web based training programs using conference calls or self-study programs will work just as well.

Determining the best location for training will be an ongoing debate and the answer will depend on your company and your channel partners. If you can't afford to travel to every remote location to train each agent then you should consider conducting a regional training program in a central location.

If your product or service represents a very small portion of the agent's total sales volume and the potential for profit is low then there is very little chance they are going to leave their territory and travel to your facility especially if it is at their own expense. On the other hand, if you are the anchor product upon which they are building their business then the sales agent may be willing to travel to you for training.

If the sales agent does not have a physical business location then the only training option may be joint sales calls with them in the field working or training at your location. It is always best to discuss this commitment with the agent in the initial stages of the negotiations so you are not taken by surprise after they sign the agreement and then refuse to attend training at your location because you expect them to pay for their travel. In many cases agents will flatly refuse to travel anywhere outside of their immediate territory unless you are the one paying their expenses.

Benefits of on–site training at the sales agent's location

- You get to know their environment and learn about their business
- Lower cost for sales agent - no travel expenses
- Fewer distractions for the channel sales manager
- You can conduct joint field work with the sales agent at the same time
- You develop strong connections with the agent and their customers

Problems associated with on-site training at the sales agent's location

- The agent may want to "skip out" of the training when customers call
- Agent may not have any inventory for training purposes
- Frequent travel for the channel manager can cause burnout
- More expensive to conduct many small training programs
- Difficulties scheduling multiple training sessions

Benefits of training at the manufacturer's location

- The agents are away from the distractions of their offices
- Sales agents get to know your company and your people
- Channel manager can maximize his training time
- Resources of the company are immediately available
- Training can be conducted on a pre-determined schedule
- Sales agents get hands on experience with the full product line
- Builds a team culture among the independent agents
- Agents may see this as an investment in their business
- Agents can tour your facilities
- You can call in other departments for presentations
    - Service
    - Shipping
    - Production/Manufacturing
    - Marketing
    - Order Processing
    - Executive Team

Problems associated with training at the manufacturer's location

- Distractions for the sales channel manager
- Expensive for sales agent if they pay the travel costs
- Expensive for the company if it pays the agents travel costs
- Sales agents see this as lost selling time
- Sales agents may not want to commit the time required
- Difficult to schedule a time that works for everyone

Piggy-Back Training with a Trade Show

Another technique that can be very successful is scheduling your training to coincide with an industry focused trade show. This allows the agents to come to the show and then add a day or two on to their trip to attend your training program. Its best to host a private room away from the trade show exhibition floor where you can entertain sales agents, have meetings with prospective new partners, conduct "private product launches" or carry out full sales training classes. This method is often more affordable for both the agent and your company since you have already budgeted to attend the trade show. Now you are just adding a few extra days on for training.

Help Your Agents Generate Revenue as Quickly as Possible

When training your channel partners you need to create a process that works within the challenges of your territories. The use of conference calls, web-seminars, training demonstrations and videos are all excellent and cost effective ways to reach your agents on a frequent basis without incurring high travel costs.

I used to manage a sales agent program comprised of agents located in many remote areas of the country. The geography and travel costs made it far too expensive for personal visits. Instead my team and I communicated with the agents frequently by phone, weekly conference calls and email. In the 7 years of managing the program I only met a few of the agents face to face but I knew them as well as any sales person that worked in my office. Even though we only communicated remotely the program was one of the few divisions that produced double digit sales growth year after year.

Your goal is to create a sales training process which will help your agent start to produce revenue as quickly as possible. If the agent sees immediate success they will be motivated to put more focus on your product. The better your training and marketing efforts, the better the results you can expect from your agents.

Here is a very simple formula to help make your sales training program successful quickly.

1. Create a weekly or bi-weekly training schedule and stick to it
2. Set aside a specific time to deliver the training
3. Remind the agents 48 hours and 24 hours before each session
4. Assign follow up work for the agents to complete prior to the next session
5. Design a standard training PowerPoint™ template you can modify weekly
6. Ask for feedback after each session – Was it productive/effective?
7. Talk about success stories and wins the agents experience
8. Create white papers and case studies that everyone can share with prospects
9. Document all sales objections and develop strategies to handle objections
10. Teach them how to sell on value to prevent discounting
11. Run a simple sales contest for agents
    - first sale of the month, most sales per month
    - first to quota (if everyone has the same quota)
12. Take issues with individuals off line so you don't waste time in the meeting
13. Respond to all agents' requests as quickly as possible (same day is best)
14. Keep the meetings interesting and stay on topic

Sales Agent Training Programs – K.I.S.S

As you have probably guessed, I'm a huge fan of keeping things simple. Too often training programs go far beyond the scope of what is required to make a sales person successful. I have attended dozens of product training seminars over the years where new sales people were subjected to days and days of classes and expected to memorize all the technical specifications for the Model 5000 Super Widget. At the end of the session the sales people were expected in the subsequent role plays to recite all the features and benefits back to the student playing the part of the customer. While these types of training programs are great for the trainers to show how well they can teach the sales people all about the product, they do little in the real world of selling.

In the first part of this training program we focused on why customers buy your product and your unique selling proposition. The best way you can help your agents is to provide training that lets them get out in the field quickly and start to see results.

A few days of making calls and hearing about your customers' problems and how you have been able to solve these problems will do more to educate your sales agents than weeks of learning "speeds and feeds" – as we used to call it in the business technology industry. Does the customer really care if your printer is 2 pages per minute faster than the competition? You are better off to find out your customers "pain points" and then build your training around the solutions you provide and the results they can expect.

Very few customers are concerned about product specifications; they want to know what the product can do to help them solve a problem, fulfill a need or create an opportunity. Sales trainers who believe people buy specifications also believe that people make purchasing decisions based on facts and figures. What psychologists have known for years and most sales people are just beginning to understand is that people make purchasing decisions based on emotion and then they justify those decisions with facts. The important point to remember is the facts come after the initial decision has been made. If they want your product or service they will use any facts you have provided to justify their decision.

If you have never conducted sales training programs and do not have a documented sales process already in use then you need to create a comprehensive selling document. You cannot afford to "wing it" or expect the agents to know what is expected from them.

> *"People don't buy products; they buy the benefits they believe they will get from the product!"*
> *Author Unknown*

Sample Sales Agent Training Calendar

		Sales Agent Training Schedule		
BB SALES CONNECTIONS				
Session	**Topic**	**Notes**	**Date of Session**	**Completed Yes/No**
1	Our Target Market – Customer Problems & Implications			
2	Our Unique Value Proposition			
3	Goal Setting and Action Plan			
4	Competitive Landscape			
5	Customer Focused Buying Cycle			
6	The Five Step Sales Process			
7	Lead Generation			
8	Fact Find			
9	Objection Handling			
10	Proposals that Mean Business			
11	Activity Tracking & Follow up			
12	Paperwork & Reports			

Other Training Consideration:

- Competitive matrix – compare your products with the competition's
- Pre-installation requirement survey
- Customer training program
- Client references and testimonials
- Product installation references

- Customer satisfaction surveys
- Installation guides
- ROI – return of investment matrix
- Shared expectations document

Competitive Matrix – I would caution you that the competitive product matrix can be used either as a great resource for good sales people or as terrible crutch for poor sales people. The idea behind the matrix is to list the features and benefits of your products as compared to your competitors'. This can help a sales person uncover opportunities where a competitor is lacking and turn them into unique customer requirements.

For example, if you sell a car that comes with all-wheel drive and your competitor does not have this feature available, your competitor may try to convince the customer that your all-wheel drive uses more gas and could result in higher service costs. You on the other hand you have determined that the customer is very concerned with safety and enjoys skiing on winter weekends. You can take this feature and turn it into a requirement for purchase by finding out from the customer what is more important to them – a very small savings in gas consumption or the safety and fun of family ski weekends.

A common downside of creating a competitive matrix is that lazy sales people often simply hand the customer a copy of the matrix and hope they see some value in the features and benefits listed. Others might just rhyme off reasons why the features are better than the competition's. They are hoping the customer is listening and is going to jump in when they hear something that has an impact on them.

One company created a matrix that was based on incorrect information and was handing it out to every prospect they approached. The competitor discovered the errors and quietly pointed out all the mistakes in the analysis to the prospects. Who do you think got the business?

Product Pre-installation Checklists – If you are selling a product that needs to be installed by your sale agents then you should consider having a pre-installation survey and checklist. These can save time, money and avoid problems for both you and the customer. Often a customer will purchase a product at the last minute and need it installed and operational the next day. By introducing the pre-installation checklist early in the sales cycle you will begin to create a sense of urgency and develop mutually acceptable timelines.

If a customer has a time-critical job that requires new equipment then you can use the pre-installation survey to create a timeline for the sales process. The best way to accomplish this is to work the customer's buying cycle backward.

1. Date the equipment must be operational and training complete
2. Date the location will be ready for installation
3. All requirements for installation – electrical, space, training the operators
4. Delivery and any special delivery instructions
5. Any customization or special needs

6.   Time from placing order to shipping product
7.   Time from approval to purchase to actual signatures and deposits
8.   Time from proposal to approval
9.   Timing for completing fact find with customer.

By working the timeline backward you can guide your customer to focus on what needs to be accomplished within specific timeframes. You appear more professional than your unprepared competitor and the customer is more likely to take you seriously.

"Mr. Prospect, when do you expect to be able to use this system in your production? What happens if you don't have the system operational on that date?" Based on these answers you can now build a critical timeline and get them to agree on the sign posts along the way. "We can have you operational on this date however you will need to work within the timeframe you have constructed in order to meet the deadline."

The onus has now been removed from your company by eliminating the phrases "it has to be delivered by" or "I need it immediately" and moving the focus to a step-by-step process that involves more than just ordering and shipping a product.

By having specifically agreed upon benchmarks you are less likely to encounter the problem where the equipment arrives and the customer's list of tasks for installation are not completed because no one knew it was coming. You don't want to send a truck and an installation crew out expecting to be spending a full day setting up the machine only to discover that they have to drop it off and come back a few days later. This wastes your time and causes frustration with your team and with the customer's employees.

> Build the value and urgency into your services - If your installation or delivery team is expensive to dispatch then advise the customer during the **Shared Expectations** phase there will be extra charges if you ship the equipment at the agreed time and the installation team has to go back later because the client was not prepared.

Client References and Testimonials – When you appoint a new sales agent that does not have customers you must have prepared lists of clients and testimonials they can use in their sales efforts. The agent should never infer that the person who wrote the testimonial is a client. They should simply suggest that if the prospect is looking for references you have a prepared list of current and satisfied customers who they can contact for more information.

Training of Service Personnel

In some instances you may have sales agents or multi-rep agencies which not only sell your products but also provide service for end users. If this is the case for you then you will also need to develop a plan to train their service personnel. In most cases you should conduct this training at your location so you will have access to your equipment, tools and in house expertise.

This onsite training gives your service team the best access to the products and begins the process of creating a working relationship between your agents and your own technical people. All too often when you try to conduct training at an agent's location they are quick to pull a service person away from the training program to solve an urgent customer care problem. Most sales agents will not have the parts inventory or equipment inventory to provide adequate support for the service people. Whenever possible the best choice is to conduct the service training at your location.

Tracking Sales Agent Activities

In William Cornell's book *The Independent Sales Rep,* Will states that the sales agent's customer base is their "most important asset." Asking a new sales agent for a copy of their customer list would be like a stranger asking you for your personal address book. A good sales agent has spent years if not decades building up their "book" of accounts. If you waltz in and start demanding to get a copy of this list you can be sure your relationship with the agent won't last very long. You need to understand that this is the reason you are working together in the first place. You are looking to break into markets, accounts and territories where you don't have any representation and the agent has established contacts.

So how do you go about balancing the information you need to administer your program with the sales agent's right to confidentiality? First, you need to realize that you may not need as much information as you think. Second, you need to understand what information a sales agent is prepared to share with you in developing the relationship. Yes, you need reports and forecasts to run your business but you can gather this information in a way that is not threatening to them.

Ask yourself what information is a "must have" and what information is a "would like to have." Then have a discussion with your channel partners to work out a reporting process that works for both of you. Another way that manufacturers and principals have been successful in building trust is by providing leads and introductions to potential new customers for the sales agents. You give them something in order to get better information in return. As Charles Cohon, President/ CEO of Manufacturers Agents National Association said during our interview, "*whatever you agree upon should be written in your sales agent agreement.*"

If you have a direct sales team then you can expect opposition from agents when you ask them to give up prospect and customer information. A client of mine owned a software company that had a large direct sales force and a channel of sales agents. The agents refused to give the channel manager any information about potential sales. The reason was quite simple. Members of the direct sales force had found out about a few of the agents' pending sales and tried to convince the customer they should buy directly from the manufacturer and save money. This leaking of confidential sales information happened a couple of times and word spread like wildfire through the program. From then on the agents didn't trust the company with any customer information until the sale was signed.

If you have a direct sales force and a sales agent working in the same territory then you must keep the agents information confidential to avoid any hint of a conflict of interest on your part. Data is necessary to provide accurate business information and you must have a discussion with your sales agents to determine what information they are prepared to submit and how often. Once you know what they are comfortable providing you need to determine if there is other information that you will also need.

Forget about asking for the sales agent's customer list. The list is their bread and butter and the chances of them ever sharing it with you are slim to none. However, there is no reason you shouldn't be getting a monthly or weekly forecast. With sales agents I suggest that you should expect a forecast at the first of the month and an updated forecast by the 15th and then again the last week of the month if anything looks like it is changing.

If, on the other hand, you don't have a conflict between your direct sales force and your agents, or if you only use agents, then you can usually get a more detailed forecast. I have included a sample forecast with only the most basic reporting information. This example will allow you to create your own monthly report and collect the information you will need to forecast sales and calculate inventory levels.

Company	Contact Info	Product Interest	Fact Find Completed	Quote Presented	Value	Expected Close
ABC Test Company	Susan Tailor 555-123-1234	Watch display	YES	YES	$4,000	30 days
Smooth Operator Inc.	Tom Jones 555-111-0432	Floor display	NO	NO	unknown	?
Simply Sales	Jim Smith 555-111-2323	Sunglasses Display	YES	YES	$5,500	45 days
Sunglasses R Us	Jane Doe 555-111-5522	Sunglasses Display	YES	YES	$9,300	30 days
		Total Forecast			$18,800	

In many cases the channel sales manager will have to call the agent directly at first and walk them through the report. Once the agent gets into the routine of providing the information you are requesting they are more likely to complete the report for you in advance.

Another way to get the sales agents to share more data with you is to suggest a compelling business reason for the need. I have often used this argument to convince an agent of the necessity for forecast and reports. If your agents do not provide timely and accurate forecasts then you have no way of knowing what inventory levels you need to maintain so you can fill their orders. If you are getting accurate forecasts then you can adjust your production schedules to be ready for their orders. There isn't anything more frustrating for a sales person than to make a sale and find out the product is out of stock. In many cases this can result in the customer switching to another supplier and the agent losing the sale.

Make sure you capture all the relevant sales tracking and customer profile information in your CRM system (customer relationship management database) so you have a copy of everything that has been collected by you and your agents. If you don't insist that your channel manager and channel partners submit accurate sales and customer reports, it can lead to serious problems causing loss of control and loss of one of your most valuable resources – information. If you do not have timely and accurate reports then you do not have control over your future.

If an agent quits and you don't have any customer data, you are going to have to start the entire process from the beginning. If you have all this information on file, a new sales agent can step in and continue the relationship without too much trouble.

How Much Reporting Is Too Much Reporting?

When one of our clients hired a new channel sales manager, the first thing he did was institute a new and very complicated activity tracking and reporting process. Every contact had to be manually logged on a call report with the name, phone number, title and full company information along with a "snapshot of the discussion." Every customer visit had to be followed up with a detailed report that required 1-2 hours of paperwork to complete. All this was to be sent by the agent to the channel manager before the end of day every Friday.

The first week no one completed the reports and the channel sales manager tried to freeze all commission payments until the reports were received. In response to the move the agents simply stopped selling the company's products and began to focus on other lines they represented. Sales dropped like a brick and the company president soon became involved. After determining what the issue was, the company president returned to the previous reporting process and worked to re-engage the agents. Within 2 months the team and company was back on track and over the next 6 months sales increased once again. A short time later the channel sales manager quietly disappeared from the company.

Reports are needed and are a critical part of any organization but the reporting process needs to be simple and for specifically defined requirements and objectives. Today with the power and low cost of CRM software every organization should have a well-planned, easy-to-use database management tool.

Even if you cannot convince your sales agents to forward full contact information to you then you should at least ensure they collect the information for their own use. Sales agents cannot afford to waste time either calling on accounts that are dead ends or chasing prospects that have already purchased from your competitors and won't be entering another buying cycle for months or years.

When in interviewed Craig Lindsay, the President of Pacesetter Sales & Associates regarding how his sales agency provides reports to the companies he works with he responded; *"I represent 10-12 different companies at any given time. This means it is impossible to do individual custom reports in the format that each supplier would like. Instead we use the CRM program.... We send the companies a monthly opportunity report that provides accurate information on our activities. We also copy the company contact person on most of the emails we send to customers so they know what's happening."*

Sales Agents Should Be Collecting the Following:

- Full contact information including key contacts
- Date of next contact if you can't proceed at this time
- Next step in the contact process
- Results to date
- Opportunity in terms of dollar value to the company
- Listing of competitive products the prospect/customer uses
- Listing of unlikely prospects to disqualify them

It is also critical to the agent's success that they keep accurate and up to date follow-up files for every prospect and customer. Without a CRM they will never be able to effectively manage a large number of accounts. Missed opportunities are usually caused when the sales person does not follow up with their contact at the right time. Nothing says "I'm a professional" better than telling a customer or prospect you will call them at a specific time on a specific day and then actually doing it. Great follow-up skills will help you build your credibility and develop trust, the building blocks of a strong business relationship.

Old School versus Tech-Savvy Agents

With the proliferation of software applications, CRM programs and mobile devises it is relatively simple for a sales agent to provide reports and forecasts with just the click of a button. Many of the old school agents still refuse to provide reports to the principal using the argument 'do you want me selling or do you want me completing reports?' These are no longer mutually exclusive activities. It is very easy for an agent or a principal to send accurate up-to-date reports back and forth without any disruption in their business.

More importantly, if an agent is not tracking their own business accurately using the latest technology, do you want them as part of your team? Your goal should be to strike a happy middle ground that provides timely feedback to give you the information you need in order to run your business. The last thing you want is an agent coming back to you demanding to know why a product is on backorder only to discover they never listed it in their sales forecast. You don't have a crystal ball and aren't required to have one. That's what reports are for.

Management Across The Miles – Building Remote Rapport

One of the key concerns of any company is how do you stay in touch with your agents and work to focus their mindshare on your products and keep them selling. A channel manager who is not in constant contact with their channel will soon find their sales are declining and their agents are losing focus on the product.

> *"The day soldiers stop bringing you their problems is the day you have stopped leading them".*
> *General Colin Powell*

It's the role of your channel sales manager to ensure this is happening by providing feedback on the relationship. It is also important that you continue to advertise and market your product to keep it fresh in the mind of both your sales agents and your ultimate customer since often sales agents are good at selling to their current customer base but not very good at developing new business opportunities.

More than one agent I interviewed commented that the principals were always complaining that they never heard from their agents but they seemed to forget that communication works both ways. If you haven't heard from the agent, he may be thinking that he never hears from you, or worse that he never hears from your company unless you are calling to complain about something.

A good practice is to schedule phone time with your agents directly into your daily planner on a regular basis. A few minutes invested on the phone can go a long way to keep them engaged in your program.

The greater the distance, the higher the expenses of travelling to your partners' locations, and the more creative you need to be to retain mindshare. In order to be as effective as possible and still maintain reasonable travel budgets you should have a pre-arranged contact schedule. This is above and beyond the daily or weekly questions and concerns that must be dealt with from the field. Remote rapport is a valuable tool in maintaining your sales agents' interest and growing your mutual business model.

Communicate with a Purpose

One thing I would never suggest you do is call a channel partner and tell them that you just want to "touch base and see how things are going." This is a waste of time and will send a message to your agent that you suffer from a lack of professionalism. Your contact needs to be planned and have a specific reason and goal. By focusing on outcomes you will create a more professional and successful partnership. If distance separates you from frequent face-to- face meetings then you need to develop a formal process to remain informed.

To do this you must contact your sales agents by phone or email and schedule a time for a phone meeting to discuss specific topics. Treat these phone meetings with the same importance as you would a face-to-face meeting. The goal is to have a standard format you use for all your sales agent meetings so you can develop a meaningful dialogue with the agents whenever you are in contact with them.

Sample Phone Meeting Introduction

Hi Tom: This is Bob calling. I would like to take about 20 minutes this afternoon to go over your sales activities and the latest sales numbers for the month. After we finish that, I would like you to provide me with an update on what is happening in your territory including a brief account of any activity from our competitors. Then we will talk about some strategies that are working with other business partners and see if they can help you in any way. Does this sound like a good plan?

If we review the main points of the call you will see that the following points are all to be covered in the next 20 minutes.

1. Review of the agent's sales activities for the month
2. Territory update – ask about their customer visits and prospecting activity
3. Competitive activity – they may see changes in the marketplace before you do
4. Strategies that are working – the wins and good news
5. Offer to provide assistance to the agent directly

The secret behind this type of focused call, which should be scheduled into both of your calendars, is that it sets up a routine for the direction your discussion will take every time you get on the phone with your agent. Once they have followed this format a few times they will begin to have the right information ready in advance. Pre-planning and sticking to a prepared format will save you both valuable time.

I have used this format with direct sales representatives and independent sales agents for years and once they realize you will be following a standard format each and every call or meeting they will come prepared. I am not recommending you only work within the confines of the questions I have listed. You should create your own format that provides the information you need to run an effective sales operation. You may determine that you need to communicate with your agents weekly or maybe only a few times a month. Whatever the frequency, be consistent. Once you cancel what's supposed to be a recurring meeting a few times you will have lost the momentum and you will have trouble reestablishing it. Your goal is consistency.

If your sales agent's preferred method of communication is email then email them an invitation to a telephone appointment. Provide them with an overview of the discussion including the information you would like them to have at hand. This takes an informal "chat" between the sales person and the channel manager and turns it into a business appointment which will have a definite focus and expected outcomes.

Methods of Keeping in Touch

- Run weekly or biweekly conference calls to focus on your marketing efforts
- Provide sales training via web-based seminars
- Schedule specific calendar events to involve the agent
- Travel to the sales agent's location on a set schedule to deliver specifically pre-planned events to drive your business
- Send out a regular newsletter or information that focuses on the sales process
- Email contact
- Product or marketing program launch webinars
- Trade show meetings
- Share success stories or case studies with the sales agents
- Have sales contests – keep them small and fun – monthly prizes are great
  - ✓ First one to quota
  - ✓ Largest single sale in a month
  - ✓ Most new customer acquisitions
  - ✓ New product launch
  - ✓ Most customer testimonial letters

Ask for Feedback

In many cases sales agents will be more in touch with the industry and marketplace than you. They can provide valuable feedback from customers about trends and buying motives. They can also provide valuable information about competitive activity. Agents can also provide suggestions for packaging, advertising and product configurations.

One of my clients was attempting to sell their product into one of the big box retailers and they had spent tens of thousands of dollars on packaging design using a reputable marketing agency. The company showed the new design to the sales agents and found out they had neglected to include the necessary product codes on the boxes. This mistake could have cost them their distribution rights with the company and may have resulted in fines if the product ever made it to the shelves.

Your agents are a valuable resource; make sure you consult them regularly.

Visiting Your Sales Agent's Location

When you do have the opportunity to travel to your sales agent's location, it's very important that you make a big deal about the trip and create a positive environment for their team members – not just the agents but their staff if it is a multi-rep agency. The trip should be pre-planned with specific objectives and goals. If you are meeting with key accounts then the agent should give you an overview of the company, the contact person and the objective of the meeting. If you are introducing an agent to one of your current customers then the same background should be provided to the agent.

When you are travelling to an agent's territory you need to make the most effective use of your time. This should include the following:

- Pre-booked appointments with key customers and prospects
- Specific schedule
- Overview of the customers and prospects you will be meeting
- Discussion of competitive activity
- Review of agent's activity and results
- Planning for improvement
- Follow up action after the visit

You may also use the time that you are in the field to prospect for new agents if you determine your current one is not producing and needs to be replaced or to meet potential new agents if you need to expand your market penetration in the territory. There is nothing worse than flying or driving across the country only to find out the agent has nothing prepared for you. If the agent believes that it's best to just "wing it" when you arrive then you can expect that type of commitment from them most of the time.

The Proof Is In The Pudding!

I can still recall a trip I made years ago to work with a sales agent in Vancouver, B.C. I got off the plane, picked up the rental call and headed to the agent's office. The owner introduced me to the staff and to Terry the sales rep dedicated to our product line. After some housekeeping with the owner I hopped in the car with Terry and headed out to our first call. Terry filled me in on the client's problems, needs and objective on the way to the meeting and gave me a detailed understanding of how I could help him advance the sales process. Terry did such a good job with his customer's needs analysis and fact find that we were able to answer all their questions and close the sale during that visit. We were both excited to have the signed paperwork in hand as we left the customers office.

This was not a "one off" event. For three days Terry kept me running from prospect to prospect. We had 2 or 3 meetings and presentations each day and covered a lot of ground. He had pre-qualified each prospect and utilized my time more effectively on that trip than I had ever experienced with any other agent. By the end of the three days we had booked two more large sales and within the next 60 days Terry closed more sales than their company's annual target for our product line.

Terry's preparation and effective use of my time and knowledge was a real win for his company, my company, his customers and his personal finances.

Joint field work when it is done right can be an important tool to help you build loyalty and commitment with your sales agents. However, if there is no planning and preparation on your part or on the part of your agents then it can become an expensive waste of time and money. If the agent wants to spend your time together just socializing then you need to look for a new agent that is committed to growing their business and yours.

Don't Hang on to Non-Productive Agents.

If an agent is not responsive to your communications and they are not making an effort to be successful then don't waste time believing you can turn them around. You are better to get rid of poor performing agents quickly instead of holding on to them and hoping they will get better. They usually don't. Review the terms of your agreement and take the necessary steps to fire them and find someone new.

Sales Tools to Help Your Alternate Channel

Don't waste your sales agents' valuable time and expertise by forcing them to develop their own sales and marketing tools for your products. I have seen agents spend weeks designing their own brochures and marketing materials because the manufacturer didn't have anything for them. This is lost time that could have been spent selling, and the result is inconsistent and poor quality materials, lower than acceptable sales and less time spent prospecting and selling.

According to sales training expert Brian Tracy, *"in sales, we now know that the three activities that account for 90% of your value are: prospecting, presenting, and closing the sale."* Your goal is to have your sales agents spend as much time as possible on these three critical activities. To do this you need to create sample documents and templates. Just as we have provided many sample documents, templates and checklists to help you save time with the creation of your alternate sales channel process, you need to create the same type of documents for your agents so they can spend more time, prospecting, presenting and closing.

The creation of standard templates has a number of benefits.

- Less time wasted re-creating standard documents
- Standardization among your agents
- Fewer chances of errors or omissions on documents and proposals
- More time to spend with customers
- Better and more consistent sales and marketing messages

Automatic Price Calculators and Product Configuration Charts

Two powerful tools that you should create are automatic price calculators and configuration charts. It is very embarrassing when a sales agent submits an order and finds out a costly mistake has occurred because they forgot to calculate a key component of the system. This is frustrating for the customer and your company and can result in loss of profit if you have to either discount the product or include a component for free to prevent losing the order.

By creating simple Excel price calculators you can ensure the agent does not forget anything in the proposal or on the order sheet. This means you won't have to go back to a customer to ask for more money which invariably ends up with the company "eating" the error to keep the customer happy.

Before instituting product configuration charts one of our clients reported that their order entry people rejected over 30% of the paperwork because of errors, incomplete information or unreadable text. By implementing the use of order templates and automatic price calculators the rejection rate dropped from over 30% to less than 3%.

There were also two added benefits of using the price calculators. First, the sales people stopped having to go back to the customers to get corrections on the paperwork and second, the profit margins improved because the sales people no longer forgot to add key components to the systems that would usually have been "thrown in" to get the sale.

If you can't afford to do the order twice then you must strive to have all the paperwork and ordering information right the first time.

Benefits of proposal templates and product configuration charts

- Agent will not forget to include key components
- Encourages selling additional features which improves profit margins
- Reduces errors on orders which are embarrassing for everyone
- Reduces returns
- Improves build schedules
- Reduces costs by doing things right the first time
- Improves company morale – fewer mistakes, happier employees
- Improves the customer experience – fewer mistakes, happier customers

Tracking Sales Agent Performance

A common method for judging your sales agents' success is based on simple dollars and cents, comparing individual sales results against all your other channel partners and creating benchmarks. This can work well if all your agents are equally dedicated to your product line and have similar territories. However, if you have a wide range of territories and sales agents then comparing them based on their total dollars of product sold per month may not be feasible.

You can also judge your sales agent's performance based on the following common matrix:

a) Customer satisfaction (using online surveys)
b) Product mix (selling a variety of products)
c) New customer acquisition
d) Market share (only if identifiable and quantifiable)
e) Price attainment – are they selling at retail or constantly discounting?

Whether you use just one method or a mix, the key point is to keep the process consistent and fair and make sure it is designed to drive the sales behaviour you are looking for. There is no point in tracking the leads to sales ratio for your agents if you never generate leads for them. In fact this will be seen as a waste of time by the sales agents.

Whatever you do to track your sales agents' performance, keep it simple and find ways to get the numbers you need from the information that is readily available. The more reporting you load onto the sales agents the less likely they are to engage in representing your product.

Here are a few common ways that reporting can be used to build your program:

1. Identify common sales trends and train others to follow the process
2. Quickly cancel or modify programs which are not producing expected results
3. Identify similarities among your successful sales agents and look for similar prospects to represent your products
4. Use the numbers to provide a quantifiable ROI that you can use to recruit prospective agents and show them past successes
5. Identify which sales initiatives are successful and what needs improvement or change

Just like in direct sales organizations, an alternate channel program is going to have sales agents who are "*A*" ranked performers producing the top 20% of your sales. The "*B*" ranked sales people will be producing from 40-79% of their quota, and finally the "*C*" ranked low performers. The trick with the low performers is to quickly determine whether these are sales agents you can turn into "*B*" or "*A*" sales people or if they are always going to be low-ranked sales people who should be replaced.

If you honestly determine you cannot improve your "*C*" level sales agents then you should quickly exercise the cancellation for non-performance clause in your agreement and look for a new partner. This partner is not doing you any favors by continuing to represent your product and may be doing more harm to your customers, your support people and your agent channel. Remember the old adage: "hire slow, fire fast."

Other Channel Considerations

It is also important to determine who will be paying for non-sales activities - the sales agent or the principal? This is a point of concern that is commonly brought up by the sales channel. Where does the responsibility of the company or supplier end and that of the sales agent take over?

This is most commonly debated in discussions about travel costs, expenses and marketing programs. There are a number of techniques for handling this process. If at any time you are going to pay your sales agents' expenses, then you need to have a well-documented and published policy. It must clearly lay out what qualifies, how and when they must submit the claim and what approval process is required. Once again having a good policy in place before the problem arises is better than having to deal with it after the fact.

Another effective method of supporting your sales agents is to establish a co-op marketing fund. A small percentage of each agent's sales are designated by the manufacturer to be spent at the agent's discretion (subject to head office approval) for their own marketing initiatives. Most often this is a 1 or 2% budget based on total sales. If you create a co-op marketing fund ensure you have a very specific policy on what qualifies as a valid marketing expense, what is an allowable timeframe for the expense, what backup documentation is required, and what the reporting procedures are.

I remember one sales agent who submitted a very suspicious looking invoice for a "sales incentive" program. The agent did not give any details but demanded payment because the fund was "his money" not ours. I reviewed the co-op marketing program guidelines and requested accurate disclosure especially since he did not get authorization in advance for spending the money as required in our policy. I later found out the sales incentive was his annual golf club membership. Nice try, but not part of the approved expenditures.

Have you completed all of the following?

- ☐ Assigned a sales agent support person
- ☐ Determined whether you need a channel sales manager
- ☐ Designed your sales agent on-boarding process plan
- ☐ Completed Coaching Exercise #9 – The Sales Agent Playbook
- ☐ Created a Sales Agent Training Calendar
- ☐ Determined where sales training will occur
- ☐ Determined where (if necessary) technical training will occur
- ☐ Determined who will pay for travel expenses for sales training
- ☐ Designed a quick start program to help the agents sell
- ☐ Created a sales activity tracking log
- ☐ Determined what reporting and forecasting is necessary
- ☐ Designed a pre-installation survey

Three most important concepts I learned in this chapter:

1) _____

2) _____

3) _____

Chapter 6 - Implementation

We all know that ideas are a dime a dozen. In business, it's execution that counts. Diets fail, exercise programs fail and business ideas fail for the same reason – most people's inability to implement and follow through. Establishing an alternate sales channel can be a major challenge for any organization. However, with proper planning, direction and business leadership from experienced channel sales professionals, it can be a very profitable exercise.

When a potential business partner sees that you have everything in place they will be more likely to become a sales agent for your company. If they know they can walk in with a basic understanding of your company and your products and leave with the tools they will need to be successful, it will be a major step towards signing them up as business partners.

If you don't have the sales process and marketing program ready to go then you need to hire an outside expert to help design the program before you start looking for your first channel partner. If you try and wing it you will waste money and the results may be a complete failure.

As the old saying goes; "the road to hell is paved with good intentions." How you move from the planning stage into the implementation stage is vital.

In the book **Beyond Performance** by Scott Keller and Colin Price, the authors report studies conducted by McKinsey & Co., show less than 30% of companies are able to successfully implement change within their organization. Not because the ideas were bad or the costs were too high, primarily because the management of the organization failed to lead the company in a manner that demonstrated that the change was going to happen. It's not good enough for the executive team to say they are going to make this change and launch an alternate sales channel; they must champion the cause, and show direction and commitment and follow through on the implementation.

In order for you to be successful in building a sales agent program there are 6 key criteria that must be in place for the channel to work. As you are thinking about your program be sure to keep these criteria front and centre.

6 Criteria for a Successful Sales Agent Program

1. Credibility
2. A repeatable and transferable framework
3. A strong, supportive owner or management team
4. Product or service differentiation
5. Ability to train your business partners
6. Defined Return on Investment

Credibility – When you first reach out to a prospective business partner it is paramount that you have a well thought out approach. Credibility is showing them that you are knowledgeable in your industry. Credibility means you follow up on your promises and execute your plans. Credibility is building trust and that is only gained when the sales agent believes you are not only looking out for your own interests but their interests too.

Without credibility your planning and preparation won't matter because no one will be interested in your opportunity. If the agent doesn't see a well-supported plan then you are going to have trouble moving forward. You must be able to demonstrate to the sales agent that you are a key player in this marketplace and you can create a winning relationship for both of you.

Is the current business model repeatable – transferable? Very often when a business owner is looking to "clone" their business model using sales agents they fail to take into account the amount of specialization or unique industry knowledge they already have. You need to consider whether this model is transferable and repeatable and then you have to create a document system the agent can follow. Consider the creation of an alternate sales channel as if you were designing your own franchise operation. Ask yourself, "will an agent become successful if they learn and follow my process?"

Strength of management – Do you have a management team that can deliver on the vision and goals of the program? All too often when sales agents are brought on board and they become successful, the company starts to re-evaluate whether the territory should remain with the agents or transition to a company controlled direct sales force. If your agents are successful, don't break it, help them become more successful. The minute you start restructuring territories or product mixes you risk the collapse of your sales agent program. Once you have alienated a few successful agents it will become increasingly difficult for you to find new ones to replace them.

Product or service differentiation – Can you clearly answer how your product or service is different from the competition and how it will help a sales agent grow their business and help their customers? Customers do not buy features and benefits – they look for outcomes. Simply put, people don't buy mouse traps – they buy 'getting rid of mice.' If you are not truly unique or different in the eyes of the agents and their customers then you will be seen as just another commodity product selling for the lowest price without any market potential.

Ability to train your business partners – This is a key point in channel success. Too many companies feel the sales agent should be able to read a few brochures, see the product in action and hit the ground running. It's not that simple. You must provide a training system to help your sales agents gain knowledge and understanding of your products/services, your competition, and your processes in order to be successful. A "wing it" attitude will not succeed.

Defined return on investment – How much money will a sales agent make selling your product? If you can provide a ratio that shows them how many qualified leads they must contact in order to set an appointment and then how many appointments they will need in order to close a single sale then you are on your way to establishing a formula for success. Expect the ratio to be different from one sales agent to the next, and expect the ratio to change as they become more effective at prospecting, setting appointments and closing sales. The key is to provide them with a program that's easy to implement and guaranteed to produce results if followed.

Finally you need to constantly review and revise your system. Creating a channel of independent sales agents is a bit like building a house, moving in and then forgetting about the ongoing maintenance – eventually it will fall down around you. Your channel is a work in progress. You must constantly review what's working and not working for both the company and your agents. You need to revise your programs and processes as changes are needed and you need to report to the agents so the communication is open and flows both ways.

When you are reviewing your sales agent program you should always be asking yourself the following three questions:

1. What is working?
2. What needs to be changed?
3. How can we do it better?

Only by developing a clear vision of what your channel is going to look like and how you are prepared to support and build the channel can you be sure you will be successful. As they say in the computer programing business; 'garbage in, garbage out.' You need to focus time and energy on your independent sales agents if you expect to grow your business.

If you view the sales agent program as a short term experiment then you better believe your agents will see it that way too and they will not dedicate any time on your products. If, on the other hand, the agents believe you are serious in your commitment to the new channel they will become more excited about the opportunity. Yes, there are substantial cost savings for businesses when you don't have to employ your own sales staff but you can't think of the sales agent channel as just a method of cutting costs. You must be investing in the building of the agent channel as you would any other part of your business structure.

Over the years I have had the privilege of meeting and working with hundreds, if not thousands of sales agents and I have learned a lot by listening to their stories and hearing about their challenges and their successes. One of the most important lessons I have learned, and I hope it is apparent in this book, is the need for any company that is looking to establish a sales agent channel to first do their homework and secondly be prepared to invest the time and energy required to make their agents successful.

When a company approaches me to help them recruit sales agents, the first thing I do is request a copy of the marketing material they will be send a potential sales agent. I want to review the opportunity, the product offering; the agents' return on time invested and understand the company's commitment to the program. If a company does not have a clear and compelling business case then I am quick to recommend they don't start the recruiting process until they have laid out a clearly defined program.

On the other hand, if the company is ready to go then I will take them seriously and I will begin to develop a proposal for the recruiting program.

When I look back on the number of companies that have approached me to help them find sales agents I would be pretty confident to say that less than 1 in 10 is ready to begin the recruiting process. Of the other 9 that are not ready, only 1 or 2 of them are actually prepared to do what it takes to develop a proper sales agent program. Unfortunately, many companies that are not prepared still begin to recruit sales agents and proceed at their own peril. The result is most of them never get past anything more than an initial discussion with a potential sales agent before the process breaks down.

If you aren't ready then you would be better advised to take 3 to 6 months to create a comprehensive program before you proceed. It's time well spent at the beginning of the project instead of jumping this step and failing.

Over the years I have frequently heard company owners say; "oh we tried to find sales agents in the past but it didn't work out. The agents just were not committed to our products." When I interviewed the would-be agents I heard a completely different story. The agents usually report they were interested in the product line but; "the company was disorganized and never got their act together." The companies that had great relationships with the agents are the ones that took the time to research and develop a complete sales agent program.

Unfortunately, most of the information on the internet that is focused on the subject of independent sales agents is quite basic and not many sources have gone into much detail on the topics of recruiting, managing, and training independent sales agents. I hope I've done my best to bring together information from a number of key sources that will prove valuable to you and your business.

As I mentioned earlier, there are a number of excellent resources to help you learn more about working with independent sales agents. I would recommend you review the websites from MRERF (http://www.merf.org/), MANA (http://www.manaonline.org/), RepHunter (http://www.rephunter.net/member-home.php and our own company website, B2B Sales Connections at http://www.b2bsalesconnections.com as additional sources of information.

I am confident if members of organizations such as the Canadian Manufacturers and Exporters Association, Interactive Manufacturing Innovation Networks, the National Association of Manufacturers, Association for Manufacturing Excellence and other organizations that are the voice of businesses began to ask for more information, workshops and training programs about changes in selling skills, process and techniques they would be quick to update their educational materials and also take a serious look at the importance of independent sales agents and their role in helping company's grow. Unfortunately, if the members of these organizations do not request more information on these topics then changes are unlikely to occur.

When I review the information that is published online by most associations, which are the official voices of their industries, I notice a distinct lack of material on how they can improve their selling processes. The focus now is on topics such as lean or agile manufacturing, employee engagement, costs cutting, succession planning, production and supply chain management and a host of other issues that do not get to the root of most companies problems, 'lack of sales.' If you can't fix your sales problems then you are not going to have to worry about the other challenges very long because your business will not last. Sales success goes directly to top line business results.

In my sales training and coaching practice I constantly see small and mid-sized businesses using sales techniques in today's market that are outdated. Sales numbers are declining or flat in many industries but many companies refuse to change the way they do business or the way they sell. As Albert Einstein said; "the definition of insanity is doing the same thing over and over again and expecting a different result." If you're looking for improved results then you need to make a change. If you don't have the expertise to do it yourself, then it's time to engage outside experts who can guide you on the path to success.

Most of the people I interviewed in researching this book firmly believe that opportunities for the independent sales agents will continue to grow as companies to look for ways to reduce the cost of sale as an integral part of their growth strategy.

Furthermore, as a growing number of large companies downsize and lay off senior sales executives, the role of sales agent will become an attractive opportunity for these executives when the possibilities of finding another six figure income is not available to them. Senior executives that have contacts, experience and resources in their industry need only to connect with a few key players and obtain the rights to represent their products or services.

In have been in sales for more than 30 years and I have met, managed, interviewed and worked with thousands of independent sales agents and direct sales people during that time. The best sales people will always rise to the top no matter what they are selling. They have the technical skills, the soft skills and the drive necessary to be successful. If you can find the right people to represent your product and give them the tools they need you can be successful too.

Ideas without action are just ideas.

AIM HIGHER

Businesses that seek external advice and information are 14% more ambitious and 50% more successful than those that do not (BIS , 2010).

Sample - Sales Agent Application Form

Sales Agents Name: _____

President / Owner: _____

Address: _____

_____

Business Phone: _____   Contact Email: _____

Company Website: _____

Years in Business: _____ Number of Locations: _____

Number of Sales People: _____ Number of Service People _____

List the main products/services you represent:

		Sales	Service
1.	_____	☐	☐
2.	_____	☐	☐
3.	_____	☐	☐
4.	_____	☐	☐
5.	_____	☐	☐
6.	_____	☐	☐
7.	_____	☐	☐
8.	_____	☐	☐

Do you sell any competing products?   ☐ Yes   ☐ No

If yes, please list those products:

1. _____
2. _____
3. _____
4. _____
5. _____

Business References

Please list three companies we can contact for references pertaining to customer satisfaction, sales and service.

1. Company: _____

Address: _____

Contact: _____ Telephone: _____

Contact email: _____

2. Company: _____

Address: _____

Contact: _____ Telephone: _____

Contact email: _____

3. Company: _____

Address: _____

Contact email: _____

Contact: _____ Telephone: _____

Description of geographic territory coverage: _____

_____

_____

Please attach another sheet for additional locations.

How do you feel this product/service can be a win-win for both parties?

_____

_____

Have you ever been involved in a legal dispute with a supplier, vendor or customer? If yes please give a brief explanation.

_____

_____

To the best of my knowledge, I certify the above information to be true and correct.

_____

Signature of Sales Agent Applicant

_____

Agent Contact Name (Please Print)

_____

Date

Sample - Sales Agent Agreement Checklist

		Complete	Initial
1.	Full Company Legal Name	☐	_____
2.	All schedules and Appendix are included	☐	_____
3.	Completed agreement reread for errors & omissions	☐	_____
4.	Territory definition and description included	☐	_____
5.	Two copies signed by agent – copied and filed	☐	_____
6.	Signed original copy returned to sales agents for their file	☐	_____
7.	Sales training schedule attached	☐	_____
8.	Service training schedule attached	☐	_____
9.	Full description of product warranty attached	☐	_____
10.	Service Requirements/Responsibilities attached	☐	_____
11.	Sales Agent Price Book attached	☐	_____
12.	Non-compete or non-disclosure (if required)	☐	_____
13.	Channel conflict resolution information	☐	_____
14.	Product terms	☐	_____
15.	Ordering & Payments for goods	☐	_____
16.	Shipping Process & Payments	☐	_____
17.	Warranties & Product Defects	☐	_____
18.	Use of trademarks	☐	_____
19.	Marketing Program Guidelines	☐	_____
20.	Reporting Procedures		
	a. Financial	☐	_____
	b. Forecasting	☐	_____
	c. Sales Process	☐	_____
21.	Acceptance of Order	☐	_____
22.	Title to Products	☐	_____
23.	Notices or Communications Policy	☐	_____
24.	Independent Sales Representative or Agent	☐	_____
	a. Requirement of General Duties	☐	_____
	b. Conflict of interest with other products	☐	_____
	c. Independent Contractor not employee	☐	_____
	d. Commission Structure	☐	_____
25.	Relationship of Sales Agent with customer	☐	_____

> This information is to be used as a guideline for creating a sales agent letter of intent and does not replace legal advice. We strongly suggest you consult with an attorney before entering into any agreements

Sample - Sales Agent Letter of Intent Template

Date _____

Sales Agent Contact Info Here

Dear (sales agent):

This letter if to confirm that you have been appointed as an authorized Independent Sales Agent for (company name) for a probationary period of _____. In the territory _____.

The relationship between the parties shall at all times be that of independent contractors. No employment, partnership or joint venture relationship is formed by this agreement and at no time may the Agent position itself as affiliated to the Company, except as an independent sales agent. In view of this independent relationship the Agent shall not enter into any agreements on behalf of the Company, shall make no warranty either expressed or implied on behalf of the Company and shall not incur any expenses on behalf of the Company.

We will provide you with specific training programs, brochures, samples, documents, order forms and support programs to help you become a successful sales agent for our product lines.

The probationary period will begin _____ and last until _____. At that time we will review your progress and determine if we will sign an independent sales agent agreement in order to continue the relationship.

During the initial trail period we will expect the following: (*include whatever you require*)
- Weekly phone meeting
- Attendance at our bi-weekly sales agent conference calls
- Attendance at _____ on line product training webinars
- Prospecting reports on _____ companies per _____
- Sales in the first 30 days $_____
- Sales in the first 90 days $_____

Commission on all sales will be as described below:
1. New accounts   _____%
2. Recurring business   _____%
3. Enter any specific instructions on shipping, warranty, credit and collection here

Commission will be paid by _____ on a _____ basis.

We are looking forward to working with you as an independent sales agent for (Company) and would like to welcome you to the program. It is our goal to help you become very productive and successful selling our product line.

Regards

Name
Position

> This information is to be used as a guideline for creating a sales agent letter of intent and does not replace legal advice. We strongly suggest you consult with an attorney before entering into any agreements

Sample – Letter Of Intent

Dear Independent Sales Representative:

This letter confirms our intent to work with you as an Independent Sales Representative for a probationary period of ___ months days. During this time we will help you become a productive, successful representative of our products. We hope this probationary period can be converted into a long-term, mutually prosperous, contractual agreement.

This probationary period is designed for both parties to establish shared expectations.

Our initial expectations are as follows:

1. The probationary period will be from __/__/__ until __/__/__ .

2. We will have mandatory communication, where we speak by phone, a minimum of once per week to discuss your progress and account activity.

These conversations will address your progress in reaching the following milestones:

    a. __/__/__: You will be required to have approached 15 accounts to introduce our products

    b. __/__/__: You will be required to attend a product training session at our location

    c. __/__/__: You will be required to attend a sales agent training session at our location

3. We must see a purchase order as a result of your actions by __/__/__ .

4. Commission paid for independent sales representation will be as described below:

    1. Commission on all new accounts ___% of product purchased

    2. Commission of repeat business ____% of product purchased

    3. _____

    4. Commission not calculated on net price before shipping, taxes..(other)

We are very excited to have you working with _____ as an independent sales agent and will assist you in your business development. If you have any questions please do not hesitate to contact me by phone or email.

Regards,

Name
Title
Company
Email:
Phone:

Sample - Sales Agent Agreement Template

For a copy of our Sales Agent Agreement Template please visit our website www.B2BSalesConnections.com and choose the link to our on line store.

The cost of the agreement template will more than pay for itself when you need to work with your lawyer to design your own agreement. This template contains most of the information you will need for the agreement. By using our sample template you will be able to prepare most of the document in advance and then have your lawyer finalize it for your company.

AT-13	**Sales Agent Tool Kit** – Includes a Word™ version of the samples and coaching exercises used in the book	This kit includes valuable tools you will need in the operation of your alternate sales channel. You can create your own documents by modifying the samples we have designed and included in the book
AT-14	**Deluxe Sales Agent Recruiting Tool Kit** – The Deluxe Tool Kit includes all the documents found in **AT-13** plus sample agreements in Word™ format	Sales Agent Agreement Check List Sample Sales Agent Letter of Intent Sample Sales Agent Agreement Sample Non-Disclosure Agreement Sample Warning Letter For Non-Performance Sample Termination Letter

This information is to be used as a guideline for creating a sales agent letter of intent and does not replace legal advice. We strongly suggest you consult with an attorney before entering into any agreements

Additional Resources

The websites and companies listed below are in no particular order. Most have the option of posting opportunities for sales agents and contacting agents in their databases. The cost varies depending on the company and so do their term, conditions and guarantees.

This is not an endorsement of any of the products or services listed below.

B2B Sales Connections – www.B2BSalesConnections.com – hosts a niche sales agent job board that focuses on the North American B2B marketplace. Toronto, Ontario – info@b2bsalesconnections.com

The Manufacturers' Representatives Educational Research Foundation (MRERF) is a charitable, education foundation sponsored by manufacturers' representatives Associations in diverse industries. Denver CO 8   T 303 463 1801 - www.mrerf.org

Manufacturers' Agents National Association - Toll Free (877) 626-2776 - www.MANAonline.org

RepHunter®, Inc. - TOLL FREE 877-895-2909. - www.replocate.com - www.rephunter.net

GotSales™ - www.gotsales.com - Phone: (877) 888-7778

Embeem Inc. - www.embeem.com

Sales Agent USA. https://www.salesagentusa.com - Phone 1-732-253-0221

GLOBAL REPRESENTATION, LLC - http://www.globalrepresentation.com - New York, USA - Phone: 716 206 8955

Reps4Hire – www.reps4hire.com -

United Association Manufacturers' Representatives. UAMR, Branson, MO 65615 http://www.uamr.com - phone 417-779-1575

Manufacturer Rep Network, LLC - http://www.manufacturers-representatives.com

Association of Independent Manufacturers' Representatives, Inc. (AIM/R) - www.aimr.net Trade association in the plumbing, HVAC/R, kitchen/bath, irrigation and related industries.

There are many other associations which have been established for sales training in most industries. Always check to see if your industry has a local or national association when looking to set up a sales agent channel.

Partial List of Sales Agent Associations

Automotive Aftermarket Industry Association

Business and Institutional Furniture Manufacturer's Association

Canadian Electronics Representatives Association

Canadian Professional Sales Association (CPSA)

Canadian Association of Wholesale Representatives

Canadian Sporting Goods Association

Direct Selling Association (DSA.org)

Electronics Representatives Association International

Grocery Manufacturers of America

Health Industry Reps Association

Independent Office Products and Furniture Dealers Association

Industrial Manufacturers Representative Association

International Housewares Representatives Association

Manufacturers' Agents Association for the Foodservice Industry

Manufacturers' Representatives of America Inc.

Medical and Pharmaceutical Representatives Association (each state has one)

National Association General Merchandise Representatives

The National Association of Pharmaceutical Representatives (NAPRx®)

National Electrical Manufacturers Representatives Association

National Marine Representatives Association

North American Industrial Representatives Association

Power-Motion Technology Representatives Association

The Sporting Goods Agents Association

United Association Manufacturers' Representatives

United Sales Agents

United States Reps Association

Western Toy & Hobby Representatives Association

Western Winter Sports Reps Association

*Always check with your industry to find out if there are any associations or directories available.

Additional Reading

Two very good resources are MANAonline.org & RepHuter.net. They both provide excellent information on the how to work with independent sales agents.

If you are looking for a good source of information about the intricacies of outsourcing your sales then I recommend that you read **Outsourcing The Sales Function** by Erin Anderson and Bob Trinkle. This book is a great resource if you are looking for in-depth reading on the true cost of field selling and why it pays to consider outsourcing.

A second book I would like to recommend is **The Independent Sales Rep** by William Cornell. Wills' book gives you an honest and informative look at what makes an independent sales person tick. Whether you are considering the option of starting your own sales agency or looking for great insight into what makes a successful sales agent this book can help you.

Secrets From The Street Reveals How To Become A Manufacturers Rep; How To Begin An Industrial Sales Career As An Independent Manufacturers Rep Or Salaried Rep by Walter Nussbaum Jr. [Book or Kindle Edition] pages 225. Four separate interests are addressed, independent manufacturers reps, salaried reps, manufacturers and rookie salespeople. All four are presented specific to their nature, yet are woven together so all aspects of the book are pertinent to the reader.

Sales Reps: How Manufacturers and Reps Can Better Work with Each Other for Mutual Gain by Bob Reiss (November 2012 - Kindle Book) The purpose of this 28 page e-book is to help manufacturers and sales representatives understand each other better, so that their relationship is not adversarial, as it is in many instances. Both parties need each other and a mutual understanding should create a positive partnership that will yield more profits for each, while extending the duration of their relationship.

How To Become A Manufacturers' Rep in 4 Easy Steps by Joseph V Leech (Kindle Book). This is a 38 page guide written by a person who has done it. It takes you from defining exactly what a rep business is and what a rep does, to selecting principals, negotiating rep agreements, finding customers, and then eventually how to end your rep business. This step-by-step guide is full of practical information.

About The Author

Robert J. Weese is a founding partner of B2B Sales Connections. He specializes in connecting companies with independent sales agents within the United States and Canada.

Robert has helped companies develop networks of sales agent through the implementation of a sound recruiting process, training programs and ongoing channel management strategy. He has over 30 years of sales & executive sales management experience. His career includes selling business technology, broadcast advertising, software, training and consulting. He has led a Fortune 500 sales channel of sales agents to major success and has a proven track record of helping SMB's increase their sales success.

An entrepreneur at heart, he has traveled throughout North America building and training sales teams. A professional broadcaster, sales trainer, fencing coach and Toastmaster, he delivers entertaining and informative seminars & speeches and has created powerful tools for teaching companies and sales people winning methods. Bob's philosophy: Success by making others successful first.

He is available for speaking engagement, business coaching, training seminars & consultations. For more information please contact info@B2BSalesConnections.com

Thank you

Bob

Robert J. Weese
Managing Partner
B2B Sales Connections Inc.

"Robert has superior communication and leadership skills. His motivational message and personal connection with an audience gives him an advantage that most speakers strive for. Sherry S.

"Bob was able to manage and structure an agent program which more than tripled its revenue production in 4 years while at the same time reducing sales travel and training expenses." - Rob M., Sales Director,

www.B2BSalesConnections.com   **LinkedIn:** http://ca.linkedin.com/in/bobweese

Acknowledgements

In writing this book I had the assistance and support of business owners, sales agents and thought leaders for the industry. A few of the interviews are included in the book and other contributions are part of the research.

I would like to thank the following people who dedicated time and answered my questions and provided their insight.

Pierre Carriere, President, BEXSA Solutions Inc.

Charles Cohon, President & CEO, MANA

Vince Cramer, Creator, DoveTail 8

Karen Jefferson, CPMR, CSP, Executive Director, MRERF

Allan Lamberti, CEO at Billiken Group, LLC,

Dane Lawrence, CSP, President, SalesForce1

Craig Linsday, CPMR, CSP, President, Pacesetter Sales Associates

Natasha Marcetic - Channel Sales Manager, Xerox

Jeff Simon, CEO, Rephunter

Greg Whittle –President, Body Guard Safety Products

Finally I would like to share with you the power and importance of today's technology and social media. This book involved hundreds of interviews over the years and using social media I was able to connect with the people who needed to be interviewed. I posted questions on LinkedIn groups and followed hundreds on discussions, debates and diatribes on the theme of sales agents and alternate sales channels. LinkedIn, Skype and the good old telephone allowed me to travel tens of thousands of miles to conduct interviews and ask questions, without having to leave my office.

Thank You -

A very special thank you goes out to Carol Weese, Susan Enns and Cynthia Hawkins for their role in making this book a reality. I could not have accomplished it without their help, guidance, feedback and editing. I am grateful to you all.

About B2b Sales Connections

B2B Sales Connections provides consulting services to the business to business marketplace. We operate Canada's premier sales agent niche job board and sales training website dedicated to B2B professionals. The firm helps clients achieve greater sales success by focusing on recruiting, training and marketing services for both the company and sales professional.

Looking for Sales Agents in Canada or the United States - we provide companies with a number of services to help you identify, recruit, train and manage your sales agent channel. You can choose our dedicated on line sales agent job board or custom search programs to help you find qualified candidates. We also have custom programs to develop a *90 Day Action Plan for Sales Agent Success* for your business.

Building your sales team? Receive a short list of sales candidates in less than 24 hours, prescreened to your requirements, all for less than the cost of an ad on other job boards! www.b2bsalesconnections.com/employers.php

Sales training that produces results in 30 days? With self-study programs, interactive webinars, or on-site training programs, we have the training solution to fit any size sales team and any size budget. www.b2bsalesconnections.com/training.php

- B2B Sales Connections -
Where Business to Business Sales Professionals Network!

A Better Career Course!
A Better Candidate Source!
A Better Sales Improvement Resource!

Canada's Premier Niche Job Board & Career Training Website Dedicated To
Business to Business Sales Professionals!

For more information, please visit www.b2bsalesconnections.com

Also Available from B2B Sales Connections Inc.

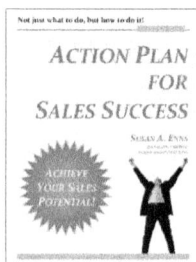

Action Plan For Sales Success is a proven, turn key program that will become the foundation of your sales process.

Learn sales techniques used by today's top producing sales professionals. Action Plan For Sales Success will improve your selling skills so that you can achieve your true sales potential..

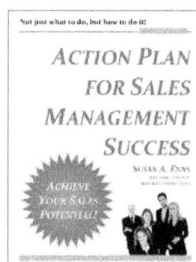

Action Plan For Sales Management Success is a proven, turnkey program that will become the foundation of your sales management process. By learning the techniques used by today's top producing

managers, you and your team can achieve your true sales potential!

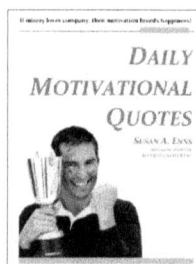

This is a collection of favourite motivational quotes. Some are sales related, some are business related, but most are simply life related. They are in no particular order, just a randomthought for each day of the year to help keep you on a positive note.

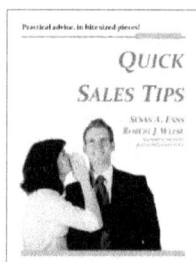

Practical advice, in bit sized pieces. Whether you are an entrepreneur marketing your own products and services, or a direct sales representative servicing your assigned sales territory, this book will improve your skills so you will sell more. They are in no particular order, just a random collection of over 100 tips to help you achieve your sales potential.

To order visit - http://www.b2bsalesconnections.com

www.ingramcontent.com/pod-product-compliance
Lightning Source LLC
Chambersburg PA
CBHW081506200326
41518CB00015B/2401